Patrick,
Always
hearts.
Love
Grandma & Grandpa

D0724119

One-Minute
PRAYERS®
for Dads

NICK HARRISON

HARVEST HOUSE PUBLISHERS
EUGENE, OREGON

Cover by Bryce Williamson

ONE-MINUTE PRAYERS® FOR DADS
Copyright © 2017 Nick Harrison
Published by Harvest House Publishers
Eugene, Oregon 97402
www.harvesthousepublishers.com

ISBN 978-0-7369-6662-7 (pbk.)
ISBN 978-0-7369-6663-4 (eBook)

Printed in China

17 18 19 20 21 22 23 24 25 / RDS-SK / 10 9 8 7 6 5 4 3 2 1

To dads everywhere

INTRODUCTION

Dads, we have a high calling from God. While it's a joyous calling, it's also a perilous calling, fraught with unexpected circumstances, emotional outbursts (sometimes from the kids too), and a clash of personalities ("Are we sure this is *our* kid?").

This joyful but perilous journey through fatherhood is a one-day-at-a-time trek. It's also, along with motherhood, the ultimate on-the-job-training (OJT) assignment in life. We learn as we do. That means successes and failures along the way, with lots of fun and laughs, but sometimes tears and heartache.

But then growing up is an OJT process for our kids too. They've never done this before, and from their point of view, it's perilous for them as well.

Thank God that He gives dads a powerful resource in prayer. No matter where we are on the fatherhood map, prayer is a great option. *Daily* prayer. Of course, we're busy men. We always have our jobs or chores from the "honey-do" jar or church work beckoning us. But no matter how busy we are, our family is our first priority, right after our relationship with our Father in heaven.

We simply can't allow ourselves to be too busy to pray. For that reason, I hope this book of short prayers will help jumpstart your daily intercession for your family. Yes, the prayers are short, but they don't end with an "amen." That's because I hope as you pray the words written on the page, you'll continue beyond the final sentence and add a few words of your own. Take what I've suggested and personalize it for your particular family situation.

Preceding each prayer is a short exhortation about the day's topic. Some of the more crucial topics are repeated for reinforcement.

Dads, to be a father is to be blessed by God. Enjoy your blessings, every day, no matter what.

PROTECTOR

I will say of the LORD, "He is my refuge and
my fortress; my God, in Him I will trust."
PSALM 91:2 NKJV

One of the primary roles we dads have is that of protector. Our children need to see in us a refuge and fortress. They need to be able to trust us to protect them as a means of learning how to trust their heavenly Father for His divine protection. The necessary protection may be physical, spiritual, psychological, or it might be related to an individual child's specific needs. How do your children need your protection?

Lord God, I love the children You've entrusted to me. I'd protect them with my life if need be. But I know there are other ways for me to protect them too: against the fiery darts of the Enemy, against the pull of the world on their hearts, against inner wounds I may know nothing about.

Father, as the designated protector of my kids, I need You to help me keep my eyes open to all sources of danger to their bodies and their souls. And as I stand guard over them, please, stand guard over me. Be my refuge from danger, just as I am their refuge. I trust in You, Lord...in You alone.

Loving My Children

*The Father loves the Son and has
given all things into his hand.*
JOHN 3:35

Built into every dad's heart is a natural love for his children. But as Christian dads, we have an additional resource: we can love them with the love of God. We can see our children as God's children too. That realization awakens in us a glimpse of love that is deeper than earthly paternal love—as important as that is.

Lord, I love my children as much as any human dad. But that's not enough for me. I want to love them the way You love them. The way You love me. And the best way to do that is for You to love them through me. I pray You'll let me see past their disobedience, past their immaturity, past their many lapses in judgment, and allow me to see them and accept them just as they are—for that is surely the way You love me.

Lord, show Your love to my kids through me.

As They Are

*Having loved his own who were in the
world, he loved them to the end.*
JOHN 13:1

Becoming a father is one of the major thrills in a man's life. Sometimes God surprises us with children who aren't what we expected. We're quiet and they're loud, or we're loud and they're quiet. We love sports, and they want to take piano lessons. The challenge for every dad is to perceive that God makes no mistakes in assigning children to fathers.

You are your children's dad by divine arrangement. Believe that, and love all your children as the individuals they are.

God, I'm an imperfect man. I make mistakes, sometimes I sin, sometimes I'm just not the kind of man or dad I need to be. But even then You love me.

Lord, likewise, I pray I can accept my kids just as they are, with no strings. No matter how different they are from me, I will love them. I will see them as Your perfect gift to me. No other kids will do. Just these. These wonderful kids You've entrusted to me. Today, especially, help me realize the gravity of Your divine assignment to be a father to these, my kids.

A White-Hatted Man

*I am the good shepherd. The good shepherd
lays down his life for the sheep.*
John 10:11

There's a popular saying, "God is good all the time…
all the time, God is good." How great it would be if
our kids held that opinion of us dads? The good news is
we can make that happen. Being a good dad isn't hard.
Largely, it's listening to our kids, giving them quality
time with us, and simply caring about them in a way
that shows them our love. In short, being a good dad is
loving our kids in a way that is unmistakably *good*. We
really don't need a white hat.

Father, in the old western movies, the good guys could
be recognized by their white hats. The bad guys always
wore black hats. Sometimes I suspect the hat I should
wear is gray. But You are the Lord of white-hat dads.
You are first and foremost, a very good Father to me.
You are a shepherd to me.

Lord, I desperately want to be a white-hat dad
and a good shepherd to my kids. I want them to think,
"I've got a good dad…a very good dad." Help me today
to demonstrate in tangible and unmistakable ways
how much I love them.

MODELING FAITH

Count it all joy, my brothers, when you meet
trials of various kinds, for you know that the
testing of your faith produces steadfastness. And
let steadfastness have its full effect, that you may
be perfect and complete, lacking in nothing.
JAMES 1:2-4

Kids need to see faith on display. If they see doubt, fear, and negativity in our lives, they will model that—and likely suffer some unhappy days as a result. But if we hold our heads high during adversity, we teach our children how to respond rightly when adversity comes their way—as it surely will.

God, sometimes I have great faith in You. Other times, not so much. But my kids need to see me as a man of faith, trusting You in every adverse circumstance and praising You in every happy circumstance.

Forgive me for those times when I'm not trusting You. I pray You'll use every circumstance You bring into my life as a way of calling me to a deeper faith. Yes, I'm bold enough to pray for endurance in the trials You send me—with the result that my kids can see how a faithful dad faces his challenges.

THE HARD PATCHES

May you be strengthened with all power,
according to his glorious might, for all
endurance and patience with joy.
COLOSSIANS 1:11

Being a dad is not always an easy road. Things may move along just fine, and then out of nowhere comes a hindrance to being a good dad. Maybe it's because we're personally facing some of the hard patches in life. If we can recognize how our present hard patch is affecting our dad-hood, we can do what's necessary to change. One place to start when we're going through a hard patch is to ask our kids to pray for us. God will hear those prayers.

God, it's been hard lately. You know the situation. You know my reactions and how they hinder me from being a great dad. I pray that daily You will show me how to react to the hard stuff I have to face. I pray You'll change me or change my circumstances. I pray for peace in our household and that the kids will look back on these days as the time when Dad prevailed against a hard situation. I pray that as my children pray for me, You'll listen and answer—not just to get through this rough patch, but to show them the power of their prayers.

Loving Mom

*Husbands, love your wives, as Christ loved
the church and gave himself up for her.*
Ephesians 5:25

A great dad coupled with a great mom is an unbeatable team. As men we're called to love our wives—the mother of our children. When our kids see the unity between a mom and dad, it's easy to explain to them how marriage is a model for Christ and His bride, the church. Disunity, on the other hand, not only unsettles the kids, but also gives them a distorted picture of Christianity. They no longer can see the beauty of Christ and His bride.

God, what a gift I have in my wife. You chose her for me from all the women on the planet. You called us to be a couple. You've given us great kids. Lord, I honor my wife in the best ways I know how. If necessary I will lay down my life for her, just as Jesus did for His bride, the church.

Today, I pray for my wife. Build her up as a woman of God. Bless her with Your presence. Give me creative ideas to show her how much I love and cherish her.

Thank You, Father, for the high calling of being her husband and the father of our children.

PATIENCE

*If we hope for what we do not see, we
wait for it with patience.*
ROMANS 8:25

Being a dad is a lifelong calling. We will be fathers to our children until either we or they are called home to heaven. During the long years of fatherhood, patience is required. Patience for potty training, patience as they learn to ride their first two-wheeler, patience as they enter the often turbulent adolescent years, patience as they find their God-ordained place in this world.

Perhaps today is a day when patience is called for as a dad. If so, know that God honors those who wait in patience.

Father, as I regard my children, I think about my hope that they will have happy, fulfilled lives as they serve You in the calling You're placing on their lives. That's a desire I do not see in reality yet; it just exists in my hopeful imagination.

Lord, I will wait with patience for that hope to be realized, keeping my eyes on You, trusting that You want this for my kids even more than I do. Bring it about. Bring about strong hope for my kids. I praise You, Lord!

Right and Wrong

Woe to those who call evil good
and good evil,
who put darkness for light
and light for darkness,
who put bitter for sweet
and sweet for bitter!
Isaiah 5:20

Many kids don't have dads to teach them right from wrong. And yet that's such a crucial lesson for them to learn. A good dad teaches his children integrity, honesty, and truthfulness. He also teaches them that such virtues will not be valued by everyone he or she meets. Nonetheless, the growing child must learn to cling to good and avoid evil.

Lord, I see enough of what goes on to know that right and wrong are under assault today. Sometimes evil is considered good and good is considered evil. Help me counteract the present culture's false values by implanting Your sense of right and wrong in the hearts of my kids. Whether it's through discussing a TV program or a current event or something that happened at school, help me be aware and speak up when I need to. Give me eyes to see, and my kids ears to hear.

RESPECT

*Show yourself in all respects to be a model
of good works, and in your teaching show
integrity, dignity, and sound speech that cannot
be condemned, so that an opponent may be put
to shame, having nothing evil to say about us.*
TITUS 2:7-8

All dads want the respect of their children. But respect is a two-way street. We need to also respect our children and treat them fairly and with dignity. We need to affirm them with "sound speech" to let them know how special they are to us—and to God.

Father, I offer myself as one who wants to model good works and walk in integrity and dignity. I offer my mouth as one who desires to utter only sound speech that edifies, not tears down—especially in the presence of my children. I want my kids to never hear something evil said about me. I value their opinion of me more than that of any other person. Take my offering of myself today and use me to model Christian fatherhood.

Being a Friend

A friend loves at all times.
Proverbs 17:17

God calls us first to be dads to our kids, but somewhere along the way as they grow up, they should become our friends too. The extent to which that happens depends on how we interact with them while they're still young and at home. We can lay the groundwork now for future friendship with our kids by respecting them, learning what they like, affirming them at every opportunity, and most of all, loving them at all times.

Father God, You are my friend. My best friend. You know all about me and still accept me. You love me at all times. For this I praise and honor You.

Although I'm first and foremost a dad to my kids, I want to be their friend too. Especially as they move into young adulthood, I know our relationship will change as they ask for my advice less often. Still, I want a future friendship with the kids that will be strong and lasting. Help me, now, to forge the kind of relationship that will turn into adult friendship with my children.

Lord, may I genuinely show them my love "at all times." May I be the friend to them that You are to me—always loving, always loyal, always enduring.

Sexual Integrity

This is the will of God, your sanctification:
that you abstain from sexual immorality.
1 Thessalonians 4:3

Surveys show that a high percentage of Christian men fall prey to porn. That sin is a quick way to short-circuit our fatherhood. We are less than godly men when we become enslaved by any form of sexual immorality. Kids pick up on stuff. They know when something's not right. If they have not discovered your struggle yet, they soon will. Learn to abstain from sexual immorality, no matter what. Use an accountability partner, computer software, or whatever it takes for you to be known for your sexual integrity.

Wow, God. Everywhere in my culture I see temptations to sexual immorality. And, as a man, I admit I'm vulnerable. But I know Your will is that I abstain from such sin and walk in sanctification—that is, I walk as one "set apart" for Your use.

It would harm my kids greatly (not to mention my wife!) for me to become caught up in sexual immorality. Guard me, Lord. Guard my eyes and help me keep my body under control, never submitting myself to the draw of sensual temptations. Help me stay pure. Keep me set apart for You—and for my wife and kids.

THE FEAR OF THE LORD

In the fear of the LORD one has strong confidence,
and his children will have a refuge.

PROVERBS 14:26

In Proverbs 1:7 we're told that the fear of the Lord is the beginning of knowledge. Why then do so many families not teach this basic lesson to their children? In Psalm 19:9 we're told that the fear of the Lord is "clean, enduring forever." We do well as dads to teach our children to fear the Lord.

Lord, I don't see much fear of the Lord in the world today. Most people, including many Christians, have forgotten how to walk in the godly fear of You. And yet if we fear You rightly, we can have strong confidence. Our children will have a refuge. Thank You that fearing You is a good thing—not a terrifying thing. Yes, to fear You is to really know and love You. I pray that fathers everywhere will become established in the proper fear of You and reap strong confidence in all they do.

This World

*All that is in the world—the desires of the flesh
and the desires of the eyes and pride of life—is not
from the Father but is from the world. And the
world is passing away along with its desires, but
whoever does the will of God abides forever.*
1 John 2:16-17

We Christian dads can easily be distracted by the glitter of the world. What is it that attracts you personally? Ambition? Money? Material goods? Whatever it is, it will likely cost you dad-hours and still leave you dissatisfied. The thing is, if we're not satisfied by Christ and thus turn to the world for satisfaction, we're entering a maze that has no end. But dads who set aside their hunger for the world and focus on fatherhood will find themselves at the destination where happiness resides.

God, I can be dazzled at times by the glitter of this present world. I know if I persist in following the attractions of the world, I will suffer great loss. God, Your kingdom has so much more for me than this world. Today more glitter will be thrown my way. Help me to recognize it for what it is—counterfeit riches—and reject it. Instead, may I draw from You the joys of the world to come—Your kingdom and Your eternal reign.

ANGER

*Be angry and do not sin; do not let
the sun go down on your anger.*
EPHESIANS 4:26

Anger is sometimes justified. It's a legitimate emotion God has given us when venting is in order. Jesus got angry. Paul got angry. You get angry. But anger not rightly handled or unjustified anger can be destructive—especially when directed at our family. We need to learn to use anger properly (under control) as a tool for dealing with frustrating or wrongful situations. And when the source of our anger is one of our children, we especially need to use our anger responsibly. The words we blurt out in anger cannot be taken back.

God, You know that sometimes I get angry with the kids. In my anger I occasionally say things I don't mean and do things I later regret. Help me deal with my anger righteously. Show me how to use my anger (when my anger is legitimate) to bring about resolution to a problem, not to become an extension of the problem.

Defuse me, Lord. Fill me with Your Spirit, the fruit of which is longsuffering, peace, joy, and love. Steady me. Calm my emotions.

Being with Dad

*You make known to me the path of life; in
your presence there is fullness of joy; at your
right hand are pleasures forevermore.*
PSALM 16:11

It used to be said that time spent with our kids could be quality time and not necessarily quantity time. Thankfully, we've realized that's not true. Quality and quantity times are both important. Our kids need the present of our presence.

One way to accomplish this is to always invite one of the kids along when you have to dash to the hardware store or run some other errand. Some Saturday, instead of golf with the guys, take the kids miniature golfing. Be with your kids as much as possible. Quality plus quantity equals a happy family.

What an earthly privilege to be Your son, Lord. Thank You for fathering me the way You do. I bask in Your presence as I walk through each day. I thank You for the fullness of joy and the eternal pleasures at Your right hand. I praise You for being in my life every moment. Be with me especially as I imitate You in being a good father to my kids. I pray they may find fullness of joy in my presence and pleasure at my right hand.

WHEN THEY MAKE MISTAKES

But with you there is forgiveness,
that you may be feared.
PSALM 130:4

When our kids inevitably blow it, do they run to us for forgiveness or run from us out of fear? Good dads are, like God, good forgivers and experts in restoring broken fellowship.

God, I thank You that I'm a forgiven man. All my sins are gone, taken away by the blood of the Lord Jesus Christ. Just so, I pray I will be patient with my kids as they inevitably sin. I pray they will learn early about the freedom we have in forgiveness. I pray they will learn to run quickly to You when they've sinned against You. And I pray that I'll be the kind of father they will run to when they've sinned against me or their mom. Lord, help me to model forgiveness and mercy toward them, just as You have toward me.

GIVING THEM THE
GIFT OF PRAISE

Brothers, whatever is true, whatever is
honorable, whatever is just, whatever is pure,
whatever is lovely, whatever is commendable,
if there is any excellence, if there is anything
worthy of praise, think about these things.

PHILIPPIANS 4:8

Kids remember many of the words spoken to them in childhood, for both good and bad. Their tape-recorder minds soak up our criticism or our praise and play back those words for many years, even allowing some of the more memorable verbal encounters to affect how their sense of identity is formed. As dads, we have the power to imprint a positive self-image on their brains. Never pass up a chance to praise your children. Think twice before heaping critical words on them.

Father, thank You for kids who do many commendable things. I pray You'll remind me when I need to praise one of my children for their excellence in a job well done. Words matter. I get that. May I trade my words of criticism for words of affirmation and applause. Help me to incorporate these virtues into my own life. Even today, Lord, I look for opportunities to commit excellence, to be praiseworthy in my job and as a dad.

Sports

*An athlete is not crowned unless he
competes according to the rules.*
2 Timothy 2:5

Sports can teach our children many great lessons. One lesson is how to win well, and another is how to lose well. We can teach them that there's no shame in losing when they've played their best.

Teamwork is another great lesson from sports. So is competing according to the rules. Dads are good at finding games and sports their kids like and can learn from. Don't pass up this great teaching opportunity— and have fun while doing it.

Lord, thank You for sports and games of all sorts. I love to play with the kids, and playing sports is a great way to teach them about life, about fairness, and about following the rules. I can teach them about the joys of victory and the sorrow of defeat, with a good attitude. As I move through life as a dad, I pray that I, like the apostle Paul, will see the similarities between sports and the Christian life. I do want the winner's crown, so I compete according to Your rules and I teach those rules to my kids. I know they want to be winners too.

Giving

*Remember the words of the Lord
Jesus, how he himself said, "It is more
blessed to give than to receive."*
ACTS 20:35

Life is made up of givers and takers. A great dad teaches and models giving as a natural part of living. When you write checks to support a missionary or when you give to your church or to the local cancer society, bring your kids into it. Invite them to give from their allowance and teach them how to pray for those to whom they give. Train them early to experience the greater blessing in giving than in receiving.

Lord, I receive a blessing every time I give. And You have set the pattern for giving. You gave me life to begin with, You gave me eternal life through Christ, You've given me my family, and You've continually given us a means of support. As we have received great blessing through Your giving, I pray we as a family can make giving, rather than receiving, our goal. Help us each day to see ways to give to others. May giving become second nature to our entire family, especially my kids.

A Praying Father

*The Lord has heard my plea; the
Lord accepts my prayer.*
Psalm 6:9

One of the primary duties of any Christian dad is to regularly intercede for his children. We pray for their well-being, their physical health, their future, their friends, and anything else that concerns them. This is a great privilege we must not pass up. Make time to pray for your kids daily—individually and by name.

Thank You, Lord, for the privilege of being a praying dad. I have faith in You, not only as my Savior, but as my heavenly Father, my counselor, my helper—my everything. I have faith that You hear and answer my every prayer—especially my every paternal prayer on behalf of my children. Give me fatherly wisdom today, help me express love to my children, and help me keep them surrendered to Your care as their ultimate Father.

I praise You, Father, for hearing and accepting my prayer.

Chosen Ones

Put on then, as God's chosen ones, holy and beloved,
compassionate hearts, kindness, humility, meekness,
and patience, bearing with one another and, if one
has a complaint against another, forgiving each other;
as the Lord has forgiven you, so you also must forgive.
COLOSSIANS 3:12-13

Because God has chosen us to be His children, we dads need to make sure our kids know they have been chosen by God to be our children while on earth. We offer them great security when they understand they have a permanent place in our family that was designed by God. Each child needs to know they are a "keeper," just as we are "keepers" to God.

Thank You, Lord, for choosing me to be part of Your family. Knowing I am holy and beloved by You is life-changing. Such a realization can only lead to a kind and compassionate heart in me. Fill me today with more of You. Fill me with meekness, patience, and forgiveness toward any who have let me down.

I pray, too, for my children. Lord, with the help of Your Holy Spirit, may I mold each of them into great forgivers, full of compassion for others and great bearers of others' burdens.

Bullying

*Rescue the weak and the needy; deliver
them from the hand of the wicked.*
Psalm 82:4

Many dads can remember at least one incident from
their childhood when they were bullied. It's not a
good memory. We fathers need to teach our kids how
to respond to bullies and, just as important, why they
must never take part in bullying. Rather, they need to
defend others from bullies.

God, it breaks my father-heart every time I hear
another story about someone being bullied. No one
should have to deal with that—especially a child. As a
dad, I pray that no child of mine will ever be found bullying another child. I also pray that no child of mine will
have to endure bullying. Help me to be watchful over
my kids. May I listen to their silent cries when they're
afraid to admit they've bullied or been bullied. Even
more, God, help me to teach my kids how to intervene
when they see someone being bullied. Help me teach
them to rescue the weak and needy—and to deliver
them from the hand of the wicked.

A Work Ethic

Whatever you do, work heartily, as
for the Lord and not for men.
Colossians 3:23

Many kids learn that work is something to endure or put off. It's much more fun to play video games or watch TV. But a good dad teaches his children how to respect work and develop a strong work ethic. Few lessons will benefit them as much when they're adults. Work is not punishment. Work is a gift.

Father, you give us work as a gift, not as a punishment. By the labor of our hands and minds we're able to provide for our families. Thank You for my work, which I perform as unto You, not unto men.

As a dad, I'm determined to pass on a good work ethic to my kids. I want them to become diligent workers who enjoy what they do, not because it may be pleasant, but because it's honorable work You've given them to do.

Thank You, Lord, for the blessing we call work.

Dad and Child
as Prayer Partners

*Where two or three are gathered in my
name, there am I among them.*
MATTHEW 18:20

What can warm a dad's heart more than hearing his child pray for him? Explain to your children how prayer partners pray for each other's needs. Enlist them to pray for you as your prayer partner, and then occasionally ask them to switch and make Mom or one of the siblings their prayer partner for a while. Praying for others builds love and fosters unity.

Father, when I pray with my child, two of us are present. Your Word promises Your presence as well. It's natural for me to pray for my child, and it's right for my child to pray for me. But, Lord, how much better if I enlist my child as my "prayer partner" and explain how that means we're to hold each other up in prayer daily. I ask You to honor such a practice on our part. Be present as I pray for my child and my child prays for me. There will be power in the prayers of a child and power in my intercession for my child.

I Can Do This!

I can do all things through him who strengthens me.
PHILIPPIANS 4:13

All fathers have days when the task seems hard, even overwhelming. But God has given every dad the necessary strength to fulfill his daily dad-duties. If you're feeling tired today, keep in mind that your tiredness is only temporary. God will supply the energy you need today. You will survive until things calm down. They always do, eventually.

Lord, You have given me every resource and every strength to be the dad my kids need. I have within me the dad-talents You've placed there. Sometimes they just need sharpening and oiling. Sometimes I just need more confidence in my ability to be the dad I know I can be.

Thank You for creating me with every single gifting I need to carry out this great role. When I feel weak and uncertain, remind me that I don't have to rely on how I feel or focus on where I seem to lack. Instead, alert me to the unique gifts I do have and empower me through Your Spirit to use them wisely.

DISCIPLINE

Know then in your heart that, as a man disciplines
his son, the LORD your God disciplines you.
DEUTERONOMY 8:5

Some dads don't like to discipline their kids, but it's a necessary part of being a father. An undisciplined child will likely have problems governing him- or herself as an adult. Rightfully administered discipline (and the most effective form differs from child to child) helps a child avoid making bad decisions. Find out what form of discipline works best for each of your children, and only discipline for disobedience (not childhood accidents, such as spilt milk). Never discipline out of anger.

God, I have felt the force of Your discipline on me. It's never easy to take, but I know it's necessary. If I learn one thing from Your discipline, I pray it will be how to pass along the fatherly talent of disciplining in love to my own children. I pray I will never discipline them in the heat of anger or for the wrong reason or without hearing their side of the story.

I pray You will show me the specific method of discipline that will work best for each of my children. Most of all, help my kids know that I love them at all times—and that my disciplining of them is one measure of that love.

Blessings

David went home to bless his household.
1 Chronicles 16:43

Many dads don't understand their importance in the family. Modern attitudes often demean the role of the father in the family—especially on TV sitcoms. But a good dad is a childhood asset that most kids need, even crave. Christian dad, realize your worth to the family. Step up to the plate and be the blessing your family needs.

Lord, going home at the end of a workday should bring blessing to my family—and to me. Some days when I come home, though, I'm the one in need of a blessing, and it's my kids who bring me back to reality. They—and their mom—are my sources of blessing. They sustain me, encourage me, and yes, sometimes frustrate me. But they are my treasure, and I thank You for them. I thank You today for the blessing of being a dad—*their* dad.

IMMERSE YOURSELF

*Do not neglect the gift you have, which was given
you by prophecy when the council of elders laid
their hands on you. Practice these things, immerse
yourself in them, so that all may see your progress.*
1 TIMOTHY 4:14-15

As time moves on, dads can expect to progress in
their fatherly role. There will always be mistakes,
but as Dad comes to know his children more intimately,
he will interact more effectively with them. Practice
does make perfect. And since dads are on duty 24/7,
there is no shortage of lessons to move us along in our
dad-growth.

Lord, I know there's really no such thing as a part-
time dad. That would be like You being a part-time
God. My calling as a dad is 24/7. I'm always on duty,
no matter what else I'm doing. In short, being a dad is
a full-immersion experience. I pray that as I walk out
my dad-immersion, my progress will be evident to all,
especially to my kids. They are a gift I do not neglect,
just as You do not neglect Your children.

Father, today may all praise go to You for Your
intricate care of us, Your children.

GROW IN GRACE

*Grow in the grace and knowledge of our Lord
and Savior Jesus Christ. To him be the glory
both now and to the day of eternity. Amen.*
2 PETER 3:18

It's our privilege as Christians to know our God. We know Him through the revelation of the Bible, prayer, and the teachings of the church. Every Christian, then, should be a growing Christian. The same thing holds true for dads. Every dad, as he grows in the Lord, should also grow as a dad. That's the irony of fatherhood. By the time we're experts, the kids have flown the nest. Even so, God is with us as we grow, providing just what we need to grow as Christians—and as dads.

God, thank You for calling me to be a father, then sending the exact children I should parent, and equipping me for this paternal assignment. When I don't know what to do as a dad, I know to turn to You and Your Word for good counsel. As I parent my kids day by day, I pray I will grow in the knowledge of You, and that my kids will do likewise. Set our family on a course that is Your perfect will for us. Bring us to maturity through the circumstances we face. No matter what those circumstances, we will give You glory both now and forever.

Complete Joy

We are writing these things so that
our joy may be complete.
1 John 1:4

If fatherhood isn't a joy, then something is wrong. If the lack of joy is due to temporary adversity, it will eventually pass. But if the joy has long been absent, then it's time to get proactive in finding renewed joy.

If the matter is spiritual, ask God for "times of refreshing." If your job is robbing you of joy, you may have to consider a change, even if you have to take a cut in salary. If there's a conflict between you and your wife, the kids will pick up on this. If the conflict isn't easily resolved, go for counseling. There's no shame in getting help. A good licensed Christian counselor is one of God's tools to get us back on track and to renew our joy.

Lord, my kids are a great source of joy, but You are my true source of joy. Your joy motivates me to do well in all my pursuits, including fatherhood.

When adverse situations rob me of joy, please remind me that You never change, and thus my access to joy never changes. At such times I need to take my eyes off the joy-robbing situation and look again to You. Thank You for ceaseless joy, Father. I need it today.

GENDER DIFFERENCES

*All that the Father gives me will come to me,
and whoever comes to me I will never cast out.*

JOHN 6:37

One of the least talked about duties for dads (and moms) today is affirming your child's gender in such a way that they accept their assigned gender with joy. Dad, you can do this without resorting to stereotypes. Not all sons are going to be the quarterback on the football team. Not all daughters are going to be Homecoming Queen. Allow your kids the freedom to be who they are, even as you acknowledge and affirm their gender.

Lord, thank You that You, not me, chose the gender of the children You gave me. You created each child uniquely and assigned the right gender. Therefore, I honor each child and the gender You created them. Help me guide my children into a joyful acceptance and appreciation for their gender. Help me establish them in their male or female roles, understanding, however, that there are no stereotypes to gender. May each of my children flourish happily as the boy or girl you made them, and may they grow into confident men and women secure in their gender.

When Life Hurts

*Blessed be the God and Father of our Lord Jesus
Christ, the Father of mercies and God of all
comfort, who comforts us in all our affliction,
so that we may be able to comfort those who
are in any affliction, with the comfort with
which we ourselves are comforted by God.*
2 Corinthians 1:3-4

Every dad goes through some pain. So does every child. Your kids have days when they want to stay in bed and pull the covers over their head. Dad, learn to notice the signs when your children are hurting. Know when to give them space to work through their pain alone. Also know when to intervene and comfort them in their "affliction." God will guide you.

Lord, You are the God who comforts me in my affliction, with the goal that I then comfort others. Sometimes it's my kids who need my comfort. Help me remember what it was like when I was their age and my pet hamster died or my best friend moved to another state. Or when I felt I was an outsider with the other kids. When my kids hurt, I pray You'll give me the right words to ease their pain. I pray I'll be a great comforter to my children when they need a strong shoulder to lean on.

A Dad's Tone

*And the tongue is a fire, a world of unrighteousness.
The tongue is set among our members, staining
the whole body, setting on fire the entire
course of life, and set on fire by hell.*
JAMES 3:6

A dad's words help form a child's sense of self. A great dad will guard not only his words, but also the tone of his voice. Someday as an adult your child will look back and remember the predominant tone of your voice. How do you want them to remember you?

God, sometimes I say things to the kids that are better not said. Sometimes I raise my voice louder than I should. Is that how I want them to remember their dad's voice?

No, Lord, it isn't. Help me to not allow my sometimes-fiery tongue to set on fire the direction of my kids' lives. Please, may my voice be the firm fatherly voice of compassion, instruction, and motivation.

OVERCOMING SELFISHNESS

*Let each of you look not only to his own
interests, but also to the interests of others.*
PHILIPPIANS 2:4

What are your child's interests? Are they interests you can join in? A healthy family shares common interests. Sometimes those interests are initiated by you as you teach your kids to hunt, fish, play the piano, or follow a favorite sports team. But sometimes kids pick up interests on their own, and you ask yourself, "Where did she learn to like *that*?" And then if you're wise, you'll shrug your shoulders and ask her about her new favorite interest. You might even come to like it yourself.

Lord, I admit my own interests are often on my mind while the interests of others—including my kids—are too easily moved to the back burner of my thoughts. As I think of my children now, I pray that I will become more mindful of their interests. Help me get inside my kids' heads so I can be a part—a *positive* part—of their inner lives.

Then, too, help me be more transparent to them, bringing them into my thoughts and interests. Most of all, God, help all of us look to Your interests and how we can play our part in Your plan.

READ TO ME, DADDY

When you come, bring the cloak that
I left with Carpus at Troas, also the
books, and above all the parchments.
2 TIMOTHY 4:13

Dad, raise a good reader—even if you aren't much of a reader yourself. Make reading time a special bonding experience, even if only with a short, five-minute bedtime story. Or if the kids are older, try reading a chapter from a longer book. Let them take a turn reading aloud too.

Father, I love to note that Paul was an avid reader. He instructed Timothy to bring the books and the parchments he had left with Carpus. As I look for ways to bond with my kids, I want reading to be one of those ways. I want the kids to someday look back and recall my voice as I tucked them into bed with *Goodnight Moon* or read the Chronicles of Narnia to them after supper. Not only will this be a great bonding time, but it will pass along to them the realization that reading is a necessity.

Yes, Lord, may I raise a generation of readers of good books—and Your Word.

Affirming Touch

*She came up behind him and touched the
fringe of his garment, and immediately
her discharge of blood ceased.*
Luke 8:44

Showing affection through appropriate touch is yet another way for dads to affirm their children. Learn which of your children respond to specific forms of touch. When a child resists a hug or a kiss, don't force it. Start small with that child, perhaps a simple touch to the cheek or a rub on the head. Invite your small children into your lap frequently…but again, don't force it. Let appropriate touch become a natural part of your show of affection.

Lord, this woman had suffered for many years and by merely touching Jesus's garment, she was healed. That's what touch does: it heals. Appropriate touch shows my kids that I love them. A pat on the back, a hug, a tussling of the hair, a goodnight kiss—all valid ways to show my affection. Remind me, Lord, when such an affirmation is in order. There doesn't need to be a reason—it's just a random, silent signal that I love them.

Heaven

The Lord will rescue me from every evil deed
and bring me safely into his heavenly kingdom.
To him be the glory forever and ever. Amen.
2 Timothy 4:18

Every Christian dad has as a primary goal: leading his children, one by one, to Christ. Early on, a child can be taught about the reality of heaven and how to be sure he or she will have an eternal home in heaven. Watch for the perfect opportunities to tell your child about the wonders of heaven.

God, dwelling here on earth, day by day, sometimes it's hard to imagine that this slice of time is only a drop in the bucket compared to eternity. Someday I'll trade all this for a heavenly home where I will dwell with You forever.

While I'm still here in this body, I pray for my influence on my children. I want to see them in their heavenly home someday. I pray for each of them that they might know, love, and serve You. I pray that they will focus not on the things of earth, but set their affections on heaven. I pray, Lord, for that day when time has ended and all Your heavenly kingdom rejoices in Your presence and is lavished by Your love.

Protecting Innocence

It would be better for him if a millstone were hung
around his neck and he were cast into the sea than
that he should cause one of these little ones to sin.
Luke 17:2

Alert Christian dads know there's a war on childhood innocence today. It's Dad and Mom's job to help protect their children's innocence from the barrage of evil on TV or in school. A child's innocence is of the utmost importance to God. It should be important to Dad too.

Father, You love my children more than I do. You have even said we must receive Your kingdom as children or we won't receive it at all. There is an innocence about being a child that You want me to protect. Our culture seems at war with the innocence in children—pushing them to grow up too fast. Lord, I can only do so much. I can't be with my kids 24/7. But You can. You can watch over them and guard their innocence when I'm not with them.

I pray for a change in our culture, where children are valued and their innocence respected and protected. I pray, too, for a return in my heart to the childlike innocence of Your kingdom.

TRUSTING GOD IN ALL THINGS

*We know that for those who love God all
things work together for good, for those
who are called according to his purpose.*
ROMANS 8:28

It takes faith to believe that all things work together for good for those who are called according to God's purposes. Especially when the "all things" involves intense family situations. Faithful dads learn that sometimes simply trusting God through the family storm is all that can be done. Trust, pray, and wait. God will work it out.

Lord, I know hardship and twists in the road happen to everyone...but when they happen to me and my family, I stumble at how to just "move on" with my life.

I know I need to trust You in all things, with the assurance that You're causing everything—yes, the hard stuff too—to work out in my best interests in the long term. You've seen some of the unexpected circumstances I've faced. You knew about them ahead of time and saw them as building blocks for the life You've called me to live. Today, Lord, I'm thinking about some of the hard stuff in my life. Help me trust You with the results. Help me see that You can take this and bring good out of it.

BUILDING TRUST

It is required of stewards that they be found faithful.
1 CORINTHIANS 4:2

What is a dad but a steward over the children God has entrusted to him? Though we dads influence how our kids turn out, so does parenting affect how we turn out as men. Are we good stewards? Do we tend to our kids with the carefulness required? Are we effective leaders? Good role models? These are the things we learn on our dad-journey.

God, You have made me a steward over my children. What a privilege! Thank You for these treasures entrusted to me. You know I'd lay down my life for these kids. And yet that's not what You've really called me to do. You've called me to *live* for my children. To be a good steward of the greatest treasure of all. Help me to remember every day that these kids are only lent to me to care for. In reality, they belong to You. I will be a good steward, Lord.

A Sense of Humor

A time to laugh.
ECCLESIASTES 3:4

Happy is the home that rings with laughter. Blessed are the children with a dad who's not afraid to laugh at himself or create some deliberate silliness for family fun.

Lord, I hope my kids will remember the sound of my laughter. I pray You will give us more opportunities as a family to laugh together and enjoy fun (and funny) times being together. Help us see the humorous side of sobering situations. Let our hearts be joyful hearts, and let our faces be given to easy smiles, unburdened chuckles, and sometimes uproarious laughter. Yes, laughter can bring healing to our souls. May it be a common medicine at our house.

Time Flies When You're a Dad

*Do not overlook this one fact, beloved, that
with the Lord one day is as a thousand
years, and a thousand years as one day.*
2 Peter 3:8

It's easy to lose track of time when every day is pretty much the same as the day before. A good dad watches the calendar and knows that his time as a dad while the kids are at home is limited and he must make the most of these short, fleeting years.

Lord, time flies! It seems only yesterday we got the news that a baby was on the way. Now we are a family and the kids are growing up fast, with each year seemingly passing quicker than the year before. This just makes me all the more eager to make sure I do this dad-thing right. I have only a few short years, really.

I pray You'll be the guardian of my time. Help me make the most of each week. Help me redeem the passing time. Remind me to slow down my life and not be in such a rush, lest I overlook important events as the kids are growing up. Never let me say I wish I'd had more time with the kids, Lord. Never.

Dad Does Good to Others

*As you wish that others would
do to you, do so to them.*
Luke 6:31

Dad, remember your own childhood? What good things did your dad do that you can do for your kids? What wrong things did your dad do that you can avoid as a father? A good dad looks back and takes stock of how he was raised and benefits from the memories, both good and bad.

Father, sometimes it's so easy to have my pat "dad" answer of "no," or "maybe," or "because I said so." Sometimes I admit to even tuning out my kids as they go on and on about something they want or something their sibling did to them that was "unfair." And yet being a dad is about being available. It's about treating my kids the way I remember I wanted my own dad to treat me. I've always said I wouldn't repeat the mistakes he or other dads I've observed made. Now is the time for me to follow through on that. Now is the time for me to treat my kids the way I want to be treated: listened to, understood, encouraged.

Open my eyes, Lord.

Dad as Talent Scout

He has filled him with the Spirit of God, with
skill, with intelligence, with knowledge, and
with all craftsmanship, to devise artistic designs,
to work in gold and silver and bronze.
Exodus 35:31-32

A great dad is like a prospector, mining his children for their talents of gold and silver. God has given your kids gifts. Find those gifts and help your children develop them.

Father God, You are the great Creator. In Your never-ending kindness, and because You have made us in Your image, You have given talents and gifts to Your people. You have given talents to my children. I see some of their emerging talents on display now, but not in their entirety. I believe You have more creativity wrapped up in my children that I have yet to see.

Lord, help me be an encourager to my children. Show me their exact talents and how I can help them grow in their gifts and use them for Your glory. Surprise me with what gifts You've hidden in my children's hearts.

RESPECTING AUTHORITY

Let every person be subject to the governing
authorities. For there is no authority
except from God, and those that exist
have been instituted by God.

ROMANS 13:1

God instituted governing authorities whom we are to respect, even when we disagree. To respect authority is to acknowledge that God works through authority. As dads, we represent authority to our children. We are, then, the starting place from which to teach them that they need to respect us, even when they disagree with us. And then we need to live lives that reflect God's good authority.

God, You set up ruling authorities. Sometimes I disagree with those in power, but I see them as instituted to rule by Your authority and therefore I respect them and pray for them. Help me teach my kids to likewise respect those over them—including their mom and me. I pray I can demonstrate to them how to honor those we disagree with even as we pray for them.

Lord, I pray that my kids will grow up under authorities who will protect their freedom to worship You as they see fit. Lord, bless our leaders!

Here's to Good Health

Beloved, I pray that all may go well
with you and that you may be in good
health, as it goes well with your soul.
3 John 1:2

Dads should hope and pray for good health so they can see their kids to adulthood. But prayer should be supplemented by caring for the bodies God has given us. Eating right, getting exercise, and avoiding stress can all contribute to our sticking around for many more years.

God, my kids need me. I pray You will grant me the good health I need to be a part of their lives for many years. Strengthen me, empower me, sustain me. Help me keep my mind focused on You and on doing the things that make for good health—exercise, eating the right foods, and handling stress.

I pray, too, for a continually healthy soul. I want my inner life to be as strong and robust as my physical health. That means getting into the Word, praying, and casting all my burdens on You. Show me, Lord, what more I can do to remain a healthy, vigorous dad.

Ambassadors for Light

Woe to those who call evil good and good evil,
who put darkness for light and light for darkness,
who put bitter for sweet and sweet for bitter!
Isaiah 5:20

We live in an increasingly dark world. A world that is hostile to Christianity. We dads need to explain to our kids why this is so and how they must stand strong when they are disliked for their faith. We are raising our children to be ambassadors for light, not darkness.

Lord, this is an unusual time to be alive and to be a Christian. So much of what we know as right is now taught as being wrong. In many cases, good is being replaced by evil. And this is happening around my kids. They see and hear when darkness is promoted and light is ridiculed. I pray I will be strong in making sure my children know right from wrong and always choose to do good over evil. Even as You help me as their dad, I pray You will protect them and give them a strong sense of right and wrong in their consciences. Help them become ambassadors for light in a darkening world.

We Younger Men

*Likewise, urge the younger men
to be self-controlled.*
Titus 2:6

Sometimes our squirmy kids have a problem with self-control. We do them a favor when we help them learn to govern their own behavior. A child with no self-control will one day be an adult with self-control problems.

God, thank You for my youth—relative youth, that is. Not yet old, but yet old enough to be a responsible man. Responsible for my family, for my kids, and for my Christian walk. To do this right I need self-control. I need to remind myself to deny the self-centered urges of the flesh. When I don't control myself and give way to those wrong desires, it hurts me and my family. My fellowship with You suffers too.

Lord, forgive me. Thank You for mercy. Thank You for the Holy Spirit within me, who brings forth the good fruit of self-control. For my kids I pray that in their presence I will demonstrate the ability to control myself—especially my temper. With self-control comes peace, and I need that peace daily.

Forgetting What Lies Behind

One thing I do: forgetting what lies behind
and straining forward to what lies ahead, I
press on toward the goal for the prize of
the upward call of God in Christ Jesus.
Philippians 3:13-14

Dads who are bound by their past can't be effective now or in the future. Your kids need you to be a futurist for them. They need you to be optimistic about their lives and how God will take care of them and use them. Teach your kids to live for the future, not be bound by the past.

Father, I look ahead, not behind. I see my future as in Your trustworthy hands. I see the days ahead for my family as good days, happy years, with Your blessing on them. We press on in the life You've called us to, looking for the prize of Your upward call.

Until then, Lord, lead us, guide us, watch over us. Show me daily how, as a dad, I can better lead my family. Remind me of the importance of forgetting what lies behind—all the mistakes and miscalculations I've made as a dad. Keep me aware that my slate is always clean, and that I can write my dad-life afresh each new day.

Dad as a Strong Man

*Have I not commanded you? Be strong and
courageous. Do not be frightened, and
do not be dismayed, for the Lord your
God is with you wherever you go.*

Joshua 1:9

The presence of God is with every Christian dad. For
that reason, we have no reason to fear or worry about
failure. We can be strong men, strong dads in every circumstance. Draw your strength from God today.

Lord God, I praise You for being with me wherever I go.
Even as I walk through the uncharted path of being a
father, You are here with me. You command me to be
strong and courageous—and so shall I be. I will not be
scared of fatherhood, or dismayed when things don't
go my way, for I will trust in You.

Today may I sense Your leading and Your presence
in my fatherhood life. May I draw my strength from You
and reflect Your great paternal courage.

INTEGRITY

The righteous who walks in his integrity—
blessed are his children after him!
PROVERBS 20:7

Integrity in a Christian dad is a must. Not just for God (but for Him too), not just for ourselves (though we benefit from personal integrity), but also for our kids. They need dads of integrity. They need us to do the right thing.

O Lord, if there's anything I want for my children, it's Your blessing on their lives—both now and in their future. Help me, therefore, to always walk in integrity and do the right thing. In my job, at church, in my community, and especially with my family, let *integrity* become a word observers use to describe me. Teach me through the circumstances of my life to be that man who walks in integrity. And bless my children as sons and daughters of a father of integrity.

Owning My Weaknesses

He said to me, "My grace is sufficient for you,
my power is made perfect in weakness." Therefore
I will boast all the more gladly of my weaknesses,
so that the power of Christ may rest upon me.
2 Corinthians 12:9

A wise dad not only knows his strengths; he also knows his weaknesses. Thank God for those weaknesses, because they force you to depend more on the Lord for your strength.

Name two or three of your weaknesses. Admit them to God and ask Him to be your strength in those areas. Teach your children about the power of Christ resting on those who are aware of their weaknesses.

Thank You, Lord, for my strengths. Thank You also for my weaknesses as a man and a dad. I know it's through my weaknesses that You can really work as the power of Christ rests on me. Use my weakness to show forth Your strength. Be strong in me today. Help me explain the value of admitting my weaknesses to my kids. May they freely admit their weaknesses and also freely thank You for their strengths.

A Dad's Wise Mouth

The mouth of the righteous brings forth wisdom.
PROVERBS 10:31

Children look to their fathers to be wise men. Wisdom comes from God. Make sure He's your source for wisdom, then pass it on to your children.

I praise You, Lord, that by faith in Your Son I'm a righteous man. I pray that as I live out my righteous standing, I will speak wisdom to my children. In myself, I have little wisdom. But with You as my Lord, I have access to Your divine wisdom. As I seek You more and more, I pray for greater wisdom that will speak maturity to my kids. Keep my mouth from speaking any unwise knowledge I've picked up from unreliable sources. Keep me in Your Word, thus gaining wisdom from its pages and Your Spirit.

As for My House

As for me and my house, we will serve the Lord.
JOSHUA 24:15

Joshua was determined that his family would not serve false gods. Today we have that same option as the true God is challenged by gods that are not gods at all. Christian dads decide firmly that their house will serve the Lord, and only Him.

Lord, our family will worship only You. We will serve only You. I pray You will let our decision result in our being a light in a dark world. I pray for neighbors, relatives, and friends who don't know You. May our family serve as Your ambassadors to a hurting world. Keep our determination to serve You fresh in our minds. May each day be a renewed pledge of our household to serve You.

Too Busy?

Look carefully then how you walk, not as
unwise but as wise, making the best use
of the time, because the days are evil.
EPHESIANS 5:15-16

Though we still live in a land where we're free to worship God as we see fit, that liberty is becoming increasingly at risk as the days turn evil. As dads, we must guard our time and walk as wise men, not as unwise men. We must make the best use of our time—today.

Father, I aim for wisdom as a man and as a father. My goal is to make good use of my time as a dad. I pray that You will multiply my dad-time by giving me ideas on how to simplify my life and better manage all my duties.

Lord, convict me of ever being "too busy" to be a good dad to my kids. Such a statement will be an admission I'm too busy elsewhere in my life and must rearrange my priorities. Thank You, Lord, for never being too busy for me.

Rough-and-Tumble Dad

Children were brought to him that he
might lay his hands on them and pray.
Matthew 19:13

Playful wrestling with the kids is fun for both them and for us dads. Outdoor games (hide-and-seek, kick the can, spud) are all great ways for family members to bond and to get some great exercise.

Lord, my kids love to play with me, and I love wrestling around with them and just goofing off. I pray that these times will be remembered blessings for them in the years to come. Help me to thoroughly enjoy these playtimes with the kids. Remind me that they, not I, will decide when they're too old for rough-and-tumble fun.

In the meantime, I believe You share our playful joy during these bonding times. Thank You that I can lay my hands on my kids without their being afraid of being hit or abused in any way. Thank You for giving me the hands of a loving father.

TEAM PLAYER

From whom the whole body, joined and held
together by every joint with which it is equipped,
when each part is working properly, makes the
body grow so that it builds itself up in love.
EPHESIANS 4:16

A strong family makes a strong, undefeatable team. As captain, Dad, you can coach the players to play as a team, do their part on the team, and play hard and fair. Make sure your team is cohesive. That makes for more wins.

God, it seems as though You intend a family to operate like a team—with me, Dad, as the captain. Each of us in the family has a special role to play on this team and the necessary talent to fill that role. If one of the team is missing, the whole team suffers. As a family, we work best together.

Lord, thank You for my team. Thank You for each one and the part they play. And as captain, I thank You for being my personal captain. I pray You will continue to give me the vision and courage to captain my family team across the finish line.

FAIRNESS

A just balance and scales are the LORD's.
PROVERBS 16:11

Remember, Dad, kids aren't very objective when it comes to claiming "That's not fair!" You're a better judge than they are, so make your determination the best you can and do be fair. When you're not sure what's fair, admit it to the kids and have them offer a "fair" way of resolving their concern.

Father, sometimes I hear the kids say, "Dad, that's not fair!" I know I've even said that to You on a few occasions. I pray You will help my kids trust in my sense of fairness, even though I get it wrong on occasion. Help me to be truly fair to my kids when I have to intervene in their arguments or when I have to assign them chores. Help me to be a father who weighs all things in a just balance.

THE WHISPERS OF GOD

*After the earthquake a fire, but the
LORD was not in the fire. And after the
fire the sound of a low whisper.*
1 KINGS 19:12

We all, sometimes, want God to speak a bit louder than He does. We just can't seem to hear His voice. But God often speaks in a whisper, so we must listen closely if we want to hear Him. Dads, develop a listening ear.

Father, sometimes I wish You'd speak to me more clearly. Yes, I'm often hard of hearing Your voice, except when through adversity I sense You trying to get my attention. Help me to listen more closely to Your voice—especially when You whisper to me. When You speak low, I know You are either letting me in on a secret or reminding me quietly how much You love me or are revealing a truth I need to know.

Thank You, Lord, that I do not need to look to the earthquake or fire to find You. I need only to listen to the low whisper of Your love. May I develop a listening ear and in turn whisper my love for my children in their ears.

A Dad's Promises

Like clouds and wind without rain is a
man who boasts of a gift he does not give.
Proverbs 25:14

When dads make a promise to their kids, they must keep it. A dad's broken promise—especially if promises are repeatedly broken—sends a message of rejection to a child. If you don't think you can keep a particular promise, don't make it. Once you make a promise, keep it. Kids have remarkable memories.

Lord, I don't understand fathers who promise their kids a surprise and then don't deliver it. That erodes trust, big-time. I pray that my kids will know I'm a man of my word. I will not promise what I cannot deliver. And if for some unforeseen reason I'm not able to carry out a promise, I pray You will give me a good way to make it up to my kids. Help me, too, not to promise anything I'm uncertain I can deliver.

May I be like You, Lord. You deliver on every promise in Your Word. Keeping promises will be my standard too.

Infuse Me with Energy, Lord

*Lift your drooping hands and
strengthen your weak knees.*
HEBREWS 12:12

Fatherhood can be exhausting, both physically and emotionally. But when God calls us to a task (like fatherhood), He also supplies the strength to perform the task. Learn to rely on God's strength to pull you through when you get tired. And don't forget to take time to rest too.

Lord, it's no secret to You that sometimes being a dad wears me out. That's when I need You to lift my drooping hands and strengthen my weak knees to go on by faith. It's then that I also need renewed physical, emotional, and spiritual energy.

God, you are a great father to me and Your energy never runs out. I pray that I will rest in You each day and draw the necessary strength to do my dad-stuff. Renew me today, Lord. Infuse me with Your energy.

Don't Provoke
Them to Anger

*Fathers, do not provoke your children
to anger, but bring them up in the
discipline and instruction of the Lord.*
Ephesians 6:4

Provoking our children to anger can lead to bitterness on their part. That bitterness can follow them into adulthood. Instead, provoke them to love and consideration through the discipline and instruction of the Lord. Plant contentedness in their hearts instead of bitterness.

Father, sometimes my kids make me angry. In turn, I say things that provoke them to anger. I know they forgive me, and that You forgive me, too, but I need help in curbing my provocations in the future. Help me instruct them in Your ways with patience and understanding. I pray I'll allow my anger to cool down before I spout off in anger again.

Thank You, Lord, that You are patient with me and never discipline me in anger.

Guarding My Heart

Keep your heart with all vigilance, for
from it flow the springs of life.
Proverbs 4:23

As men in today's society, we face many attacks on our roles as fathers. For instance, on TV, Dad is frequently demeaned or given only a cameo role in the lives of his children. If we accept the world's increasingly minimalist role of fatherhood, our kids will pay the price. As dads, we need to know who we are and what we're about. We are to keep our father-hearts with all vigilance. God has placed much there that He wants us to use as we raise our children.

God, what You've put in my heart is priceless. You chose me as Your child and You've given me much to oversee in these few short years I have on earth. I pray that I'll pay better attention to the issues that flow out of my heart—the springs of life You have for me. Keep me centered, Lord. Keep me on track in all I do—as a man, a worker, a dreamer, a husband, a Christian, and a father. Let my fathering talents flow today from a heart kept with vigilance.

DOING GOD'S WILL

*Be doers of the word, and not hearers
only, deceiving yourselves.*
JAMES 1:22

Dads have special ways of "doing" (not just hearing) God's Word. The doing involves training our children, praying with them, playing with them, providing for them, and making them secure. This is God's will for us. It's what God wants us dads to *do*.

Father, help me to be a doer of Your will with my whole self, not just someone who hears with my ears. Help me put feet to my faith—especially in the lives of my kids. Your will for me as their father is to do right by them. To make You known to them by my words and actions by doing what Your Word says.

Lord, help me make Your will, my will. Help me make Your priorities, my priorities. And help me demonstrate to my children what doing Your will looks like.

A Dad's Tears

*You have kept count of my tossings; put my tears
in your bottle. Are they not in your book?*
PSALM 56:8

One mark of a Christian is joy, but there will also be sorrows during the course of a lifetime. For dads, the sorrows could come from the serious illness or death of a child, rebellion during the teen years, a broken marriage, or perhaps a job loss. Dads shed tears. But God sees when dads cry. He puts our "tears in a bottle." He understands our every heartache.

Sometimes we men do cry—or feel the need to. Lord, in many ways You've granted me success, and for that I thank You. But some days I seem to focus on my failures or the pain from my past—or even from my present—or from my kids.

Lord, You know the source of my tears. You have even kept count of the tears I've cried—yeah, some of which have been invisible. I pray that these tears will not have been shed in vain. I pray you will use my pain to strengthen me and to give me a heart of compassion for others, especially compassion for my children when they're hurting. You are my Healer and my Comforter. I trust in You today as You consider my pain.

Obedient Children and Fair-Minded Parents

*Children, obey your parents in
the Lord, for this is right.*
Ephesians 6:1

Obedient children and fair-minded parents make for a happy family. Obedience, though, is not inborn in our children. Obedience must be taught by Mom and Dad and learned by the child. This takes time and practice, but the payoff is worth it.

Father, teaching my kids to obey instantly isn't easy. They're often slow to follow through and they sometimes question my directives. Yet I know when I look in the mirror, I see a man who isn't always instantly (and cheerfully) obedient to Your directives, even though You mean them for my own good, just as I mean them for my children's own good

Help me as a dad to first be obedient to You—for "this is right." Then help me be the kind of dad whose directives can be trusted by his children. And Lord, may we all see the fruit of obedience—a happy, peaceful, productive life.

FELLOWSHIP WITH OTHER DADS

Iron sharpens iron, and one man sharpens another.
PROVERBS 27:17

Dads need to hang out with other dads often. By talking and comparing notes, dads can hear what has worked and what hasn't with other men. Find ways to both exchange information and have some fun with other dads. Your kids will reap the benefits.

Lord, fatherhood is so much easier when I get together with other guys who are traveling the dad-path. I need more input, though, from my fellow travelers. I pray for Christian fathers everywhere, but especially the ones I know and with whom I enjoy fellowship. I pray for closer friendships with other dads, knowing that not only will I benefit, but so will my children.

Father, I need to sharpen myself with other dads. Open up opportunities for this to happen.

The Danger of High Places

Solomon loved the Lord, walking in the statutes of David his father, only he sacrificed and made offerings at the high places.
1 Kings 3:3

The "high places" in the Old Testament were where the enemies of Israel worshiped their foreign gods. Knowing such places of false worship would be a trap for His people, God commanded the Israelites to tear down the "high place" altars. Solomon, King David's son, started off well with the Lord, but then he disobeyed Him and took to himself foreign wives who turned his heart away, after other gods.

As your children grow, they will face many foreign gods in our culture. There will be high place altars to which they may be tempted to turn. This must not be. As a father, pray and protect your children from the attraction of false gods.

Lord God! What a mess Solomon made of his life by turning from You. Father, I pray for my kids. I ask You to protect them from the lure of our culture's false ideologies that, when followed, bring only disaster. I pray, too, that You will keep me from such idolatry. I pray for my descendants for generations. Keep our lineage true to You, O God!

Reproving Your Child

*The LORD reproves him whom he loves, as
a father the son in whom he delights.*
PROVERBS 3:12

One proof that we love our kids is our willingness to "reprove" them when they need it. If we delight in our children, we will lovingly discipline them.

God, it hurts when I have to discipline my kids. Yet I can look at my own childhood and see how good discipline helped me become a better man and poor discipline only discouraged me or made me bitter. Love disciplines, even when it's hard. You discipline me, and although it does me good, it also hurts. I take comfort in the fact that You discipline me because You delight in me. Likewise, may my disciplining my children be only a response to my delight in them. May I never discipline them because I had a bad day or I didn't take time to learn all the facts.

Lord, help me be a wise discipliner.

Worthy of Honor

Honor your father and mother.
Matthew 19:19

God places value on parenthood and expects us to value it as well. Every dad has or has had parents. We dads need to be not only worthy of the honor of our children, but we need to honor our own parents as well, even if that's hard to do.

Today, take a moment to remember the best times with your parents. Forget the other times.

God, I've seen some dads who are not worthy of being honored. They are distant from their kids, emotionally or physically or both. I know that hurts the children in many ways. Help me be a dad worthy of honor. Help me do the right things and say the right things to ensure that my children know how much I care for them.

And, Lord, help me honor my own parents. Times weren't always great growing up, but even so, now that I'm a dad, I understand a bit more of what my own dad went through. I applaud and honor his positive efforts and forgive his lapses. Thank You that, in both cases, he has been a lesson in what to do and what not to do as a dad.

A Father's Everlasting Love

The steadfast love of the LORD is from everlasting
to everlasting on those who fear him, and
his righteousness to children's children.
PSALM 103:17

It's hard for us to fathom God's everlasting love for us. Our minds just can't grasp the infinite and intense love of God for His people. Our love for our children is only a teaspoon measurement of that love. Today, that love is lavished on you, so live as one who is loved steadfastly by your heavenly Father.

God, I love my children, but it boggles my mind that Your everlasting love is even greater. Your love and Your righteousness extend past me and on to my children. We are the object of Your everlasting love. I pray we will never forget, underestimate, or take for granted Your love, but that we will thrive on it.

Lord, we fear You as we love You. In Your great love we take cover from the assaults of the Enemy and the rejection from the world. Keep us forever in Your love.

Sexual Boundaries

*I say to you that everyone who looks at a
woman with lustful intent has already
committed adultery with her in his heart.*
Matthew 5:28

God has designed us men to be monogamous and
faithful to the wife He has given us. Some Christian men have ruined their lives by following their wandering eyes to an adulterous encounter. But you can resolve daily to love your wife. You can turn your eyes away from temptations that will destroy your family. Don't let it happen.

Lord, it's true. I sometimes have a problem with wandering eyes. You know only too well how I sometimes struggle to keep a pure mind. But what's more dangerous to a strong family than to have a dad who strays (even in thought) from loyalty to his wife and children?

God, I repent from my lust and want to keep my sexual desires directed only toward loving and caring for my wife and being a great dad to the kids. Cleanse me from my sexual sins and show me ways to effectively keep a pure mind in the midst of an impure culture.

Help all us dads with this problem, Lord.

Obedience

*I do as the Father has commanded me, so that
the world may know that I love the Father.*
John 14:31

If we are to see obedient children, we men must learn
to be obedient to God.

God, now that I'm a dad, I understand more about
obedience than I did when I was a son. I remember
how hard it was to obey when I wanted my own way in
a matter. Now I see my own kids struggling to obey at
times. And yet Jesus obeyed so the world would know
He loved the Father. That's what obedience to a parent is: showing your love through doing the very things
that a loving father has commanded.

Lord, it's not too late for me to show my love by
being obedient. Help me impress on my children why
obedience is so important, even when it goes against
our own desires.

FATHERLY LOVE

May our Lord Jesus Christ himself, and God our
Father, who loved us and gave us eternal comfort
and good hope through grace, comfort your hearts
and establish them in every good work and word.
2 THESSALONIANS 2:16-17

Being a dad is part of our assigned "good work." May God establish each of us as the successful father we need to be.

Thank You, Father, for grace that brings me comfort and hope. By Your grace I'm established in every good work and word, including my role as a father. Thank You for the grace that comes to me because of Your love for me. Your overwhelming fatherly love empowers me daily. I praise You, Lord, as I grow daily in Your love.

DADS ARE KIDS TOO

*See what kind of love the Father has
given to us, that we should be called
children of God; and so we are.*

1 JOHN 3:1

Sometimes we dads forget that we, too, are children
with a father. We are recipients of the kind of love
only God can give. And then we are givers of the kind
of love that our children need. Through living in God's
love, we are able to be the right father for every child
He has given us.

Lord, sometimes I forget You're a father too. Like me,
You have children You parent. In fact, I'm one of Your
children, born again into Your kingdom to become heir
to a great inheritance. Your love has done this. Your
love that knew me before I was born. Your love that
reaches down to me today from eternity past. God,
thank You for this unfathomable father-love that has
made me a child of Yours. Today may I reflect Your
love as the perfect father to my kids. May I be the right
father for every child of mine.

Walking in Truth

I rejoiced greatly to find some of your
children walking in the truth, just as
we were commanded by the Father.
2 John 1:4

Teaching our kids the truth and how to walk in it is part of our assignment as dads. To do that, we must ourselves walk in the truth of God's Word. We teach truth by modeling truth.

Lord, all parents want their children to walk in the truth. You sure do. So do I. The kids today are exposed to so many lies in our culture. As they subtly accept these lies as truth, their paths go crooked and they might never end up at their rightful goal.

God, help the kids—all of the next generation, but especially mine. I, like the apostle John, will rejoice greatly to know my children are walking in the truth of Your Word and finding a straight path for their young feet.

Kingdom Wisdom

*Set your minds on things that are above,
not on things that are on earth.*
Colossians 3:2

A dad with a heavenly mind-set will be more effective here on earth. Why? Because he has his priorities in order. When you know what really matters, what really comes first, all the rest falls into place. Stay focused on things above—and on doing God's will. Success will be yours.

Lord, some days it's hard not to be concerned with the "things that are on earth." Yet you call me as a man and as a dad to something greater, something higher. You call me to be part of Your kingdom, even while I live out this earthly life. As I seek first Your kingdom, I'll find the things of earth "strangely dim," as the old hymn puts it. I'll also find, as is revealed in Matthew 6:33, that if I seek first Your kingdom, all my earthly needs—food, drink, clothing—will be added to me.

Father, Your kingdom has first place in my life. Your kingdom informs the way I parent my kids. Thank You for kingdom wisdom as a dad.

When God Seems Distant

*Be strong and courageous. Do not fear or be in
dread of them, for it is the L*ORD *your God who
goes with you. He will not leave you or forsake you.*
DEUTERONOMY 31:6

Sometimes days or even weeks will pass when we
don't sense God's activity in our life. But we know
we can't go by how we feel or what our senses tell us.
We go by God's promises. We move ahead as dads by
knowing that the Lord our God goes with us. He will
not leave us or forsake us.

Lord, when our first child was born, we entered into
a different land. It was scary then, and it still is sometimes. Thank You that when my wife and I entered this
strange new land of parenthood, You were with us. You
are still with us—every step of the way, and necessarily so.

We don't always sense Your presence, Lord.
Sometimes it seems like we're doing this parenting
journey on our own. And yet, You are there. Abundantly
there. You have not left us or forsaken us.

In You, Lord, I am a strong and courageous dad.
With Your help, I can handle anything.

Contentedness

Godliness with contentment is great gain, for we
brought nothing into the world, and we cannot
take anything out of the world. But if we have food
and clothing, with these we will be content. But
those who desire to be rich fall into temptation, into
a snare, into many senseless and harmful desires
that plunge people into ruin and destruction. For
the love of money is a root of all kinds of evils.
1 Timothy 6:6-10

As the old saying goes, "You can't take it with you." Good dads resist following the love of money. Money can't turn out happy and well-adjusted, God-serving kids. But you can, if you make having emotionally and spiritually rich kids your goal, not having a hefty bank account.

Lord, I hold out my empty hands and ask You to fill them. I have nothing that has not come first from You. I have nothing that will follow me out of this world. Because of this, I'm content in pursuing godliness and obtaining great gain.

Father, I focus on eternity and the one thing that can follow me there—godly kids who love and serve You. There is nothing more important to me than that my children follow You. With this, I am content.

The Living God

My soul thirsts for God, for the living God.
PSALM 42:2

The God we serve is a living God. He is with us and quenches our thirst. Because we serve a living God, we have no fears of what man or earthly circumstances can do. We are confident fathers because the living God has equipped us to be the exact father our children need. How then can we not thirst after such a God?

Lord, I worship You today as the living God, sovereign over all the earth. Sovereign over my life and the lives of my children. You live—and You give life to those who love You. I pray that this life I live as a dad will be infused with Your living life. I can't manufacture the kind of life I should live—but I can allow You to live Your life through me. Live in me as I father, as I love my wife, as I work at my job.

Today, Father, my soul thirsts for You. And I bow down to You and praise You for the life You give me. True life.

LIVING FOR THE GLORY OF GOD

Whatever you do, do all to the glory of God.
1 CORINTHIANS 10:31

When we think about being a dad "to the glory of God," we can see how crucial our parenting is to God. Today, be a dad to the glory of God.

Lord, my prayer is that I am a dad "to the glory of God." Raising great kids is good, but it's not enough if my children never grasp living for You. As I interact with my kids, help me to remember that my goal is to be a dad "to the glory of God."

Lord, I praise You for the children You've given me. May they, too, do all to the glory of God.

Keeping Myself in
the Love of God

*You, beloved, building yourselves up in your most
holy faith and praying in the Holy Spirit, keep
yourselves in the love of God, waiting for the mercy
of our Lord Jesus Christ that leads to eternal life.*
Jude 20-21

As we dads live out our paternal role, we can do
so keeping ourselves in the love of God. That is,
reminding ourselves that God's love is what guides us
and sustains us as dads. We build ourselves up in the
faith as we daily pray in the Holy Spirit and read God's
Word. In so doing, we become stronger men and better
dads.

Thank You, God, for Your love for me. Thank You for the
opportunity to build myself up in the faith by praying in
the Holy Spirit and reading Your Word. I keep not only
myself in Your love, but by faith, I keep my family there
too.

Lord, we belong to You—all of us. We look ahead
past this present life to an eternity in Your presence.
Thank You for Your mercy. Thank You for grace. Thank
You for this day as a dad and all that it holds. I praise
You, Lord!

Every Child Is a Child with Special Needs

We who are strong have an obligation to bear with the failings of the weak, and not to please ourselves.
ROMANS 15:1

Every Christian man has an obligation to bear with the failings of the weak. As dads, sometimes it's our own children who are weak, who have special needs. Who better than us to be there for them, bearing their weakness with them? When a dad does this, he himself becomes stronger.

Father, so many kids have obvious special needs. Some are severely challenged, others less so. But Lord, help me to see that every child has special needs. Each of my children has emotional, physical, and spiritual needs that I, as their dad, must recognize and see that those needs are met. Right now I think of each of my children and the specific needs I know about in their lives. Show me how to meet those needs. Show me how to give them confidence to make full use of their strengths and not focus on their weaknesses.

Remember, too, Lord, that I'm one of Your children with special needs. I pray You'll meet those needs only You and I know about.

Dad-Hood Is an OJT Event

Let the wise hear and increase in learning, and
the one who understands obtain guidance.
PROVERBS 1:5

Dads may start without much know-how in the parenting business, but slowly, day by day, week by week, year by year, the knowledge and experience accumulates. As dads, we build on what we learned last week. And so it goes. If we're wise dads, we will hear and increase in learning as God brings fresh parenting circumstances our way. We can benefit from our gained experience.

God, this fatherhood thing is still "on-the-job" training for me. Paternity 101 was not a class offered in school. But I'm listening as You teach me. I'm learning as I go. And I'm looking to You and to some of my fellow fathers for guidance. I pray You'll help me be a fast learner and that my dad-mistakes won't hurt my kids. Teach me, Lord. I'm willing to learn more.

DEVELOPING A FATHER-HEART

*He will turn the hearts of fathers to their children
and the hearts of children to their fathers.*
MALACHI 4:6

God can only turn hearts that are malleable. He can do little with hard hearts. Let's allow God to mold our hearts, turning them to our children and watching as He turns their hearts to us.

Lord, it seems fathering doesn't come naturally to a lot of us dads. At least not the entirety of fathering kids right. We want to do right, but sometimes we miss the mark. But You can give us a father-heart. You can turn our hearts fully to our children and theirs to us. You can bond us with our children so well that the bond can be broken only at the grave.

I need a father-heart, God. I need You to reinforce the bond I have with my kids. Bring us closer. Help us love more effectively. Help us love like You love.

A Good Man

The steps of a good man are ordered by the
Lord: and he delighteth in his way.
Psalm 37:23 kjv

When we realize that our steps are ordered of the Lord—and that He delights in our way—we can be confident fathers. We can trust Him to order our steps rightly and to the advantage of our children. God cares that much for us.

Today, Lord, I look to You to delight in my way. No, I'm not "good" on my own account; I'm good in that I love You as my Father, follow Christ as my Savior, and am led by the Holy Spirit. All my goodness, then, comes from You, not from me or anything I do. And yet, for such as me, Your promise is to order my steps today. And as I fulfill my duties as a dad, I especially pray for You to order my paternal steps. I pray You'll help me as I interact with my kids. Help me to have patience, to show them kindness, and to teach them how to be "good" by following You, so that their steps, too, might be ordered by You.

Dad as Servant

*As each has received a gift, use it to serve one
another, as good stewards of God's varied grace.*
1 Peter 4:10

Because God has called men to be the head of the
household, we sometimes get the wrong idea that
God thinks more highly of us. The opposite is true. To
be the head of the family is not to be the boss of the
family, but to be the servant of the family. We serve by
leading. We serve through humility. We are thus stewards of God's grace in our family circle.

Lord, I see my role as a father as that of a servant to
my kids. I'm serving them by praying for them, teaching
them, and doing things for them they're not old enough
to do for themselves. This servant role is something I
do as a steward of Your grace and as a guardian over
the children You've entrusted to me.

These children are a gift, Lord, and I don't forget
that. Help me to serve them well.

DAD AS SPIRITUAL MENTOR

I will instruct you and teach you in the way you should go; I will counsel you with my eye upon you.
PSALM 32:8

One thing dads can depend on is that God has a vested interest in their success as fathers. God has ordained fathers to instruct and teach their children in the way they should go, just as He promises to instruct and teach all Christians in the way they should go. That's part of God's role as our heavenly Father. And part of our role as earthly fathers is to likewise counsel our children with our eyes upon them, meaning that we carefully watch over them. If we don't instruct, teach, and counsel our kids, someone else will. And that someone may not direct our children rightly.

Father God, I know one of Your purposes in instructing me, in teaching me in the way I should go, is that I can do likewise for my children. When they see me, it's very likely they will get a picture of what You're like. That amazes me...and terrifies me a little. Yet as You counsel me, I will counsel them in the way they should go. As You keep Your eye on me, so will I keep my eyes on You. Even now, God, I'm overcome with the knowledge of Your eye—and hand—upon my life. It's sobering...and strengthening.

My Child's Friends

My son, if sinners entice you, do not consent.
PROVERBS 1:10

At some point every child will be invited into a friendship with someone who has a different set of values. Some potential friends may have no good values at all. A dad needs to be aware of his children's friends and make sure that if there's any influencing going on, it's his son or daughter doing the influencing. It's a mistake to allow our children to come under the influence of "friends" who would entice them to evil.

Lord, I want my children to have good friends. But nowadays, it's hard to know if all their friends are safe friends. Sometimes I worry about "sleepovers" or outings my kids might take with other families. God, You're going to have to give me discernment and the courage to say no when I have a gut feeling that something's not right. I pray, too, that You'll help me teach my kids to be leaders, not followers, so they are not easily enticed by friends into sinful situations. I pray my kids will be a good influence on their friends, not be influenced wrongly by their friends.

TRAINING THEIR EYES

I will set no wicked thing before mine eyes.
PSALM 101:3 KJV

The eyes are an entry point for our thought life. What we see influences what we think. What we think influences what we do. To look at evil is to take it into our minds. We shouldn't do this ourselves, nor should we allow our children to dabble with evil, even with viewing evil.

Lord, sometimes it's discouraging to see all the tempting images put before not only my vulnerable eyes, but the eyes of my kids too. How can I possibly shield them from all the impure images that will be embeded in their minds for years? Images that feed their fallen nature in such a way as to ensnare them into a life of bondage to sin.

Help me, as I am their role model, to "set no wicked thing" before my own eyes. Remind me to keep them and their innocence before You in prayer. Guard them from evil, Lord. Direct them, in part through my example, to seek only good, not evil.

A "No-Excuses" Dad

But they all alike began to make excuses.
LUKE 14:18

It takes courage to own up to our mistakes, but to do so shows we are responsible men. Let's set an example for the kids. No lame excuses.

Father, sometimes I justify my dad-mistakes. I come up with some pretty good excuses. Some, though, aren't so good. They're just meant to get me off the hook. Lord, I know that's not a good example. I need to become more of a "no-excuses" dad. Help me take responsibility when I make a mistake or do something I shouldn't. Help me raise kids who won't allow themselves the luxury of excuses when they mess up.

Overcoming Shame

*Those who look to him are radiant, and
their faces shall never be ashamed.*

Psalm 34:5

God sets us free from all shame. And that is a great freedom. Shame accomplishes nothing. It only tears us down. Instead, let's get rid of shame, look to God, and be radiant.

Lord, I've known shame in my life. Sometimes I know it still. But You are the God who releases people from shame. You are the one to whom I can look without shame and be radiant. Why? Because all my shame and all that has caused my shame was fully dealt with on the cross. Whatever shame remains with me, I now place there on the cross with Christ and leave it forever behind.

I pray, too, Father, that I will never shame my kids. Correct them, yes. Discipline them, of course. But pour shame on them, no. Instead, help me teach my kids how to take whatever shame they have straight to the cross and receive release. May they, too, know the radiance of a life without shame.

Father/Child Retreats

He said to them, "Come away by yourselves
to a desolate place and rest a while."
Mark 6:31

Each child who calls us "Dad" deserves time alone with us. Such personal outings will become a lifetime memory for both Dad and the child. Don't forget to have an occasional Dad/Mom retreat too.

Father, it's good to get away sometimes. I need to have father/child experiences with my kids—just me and them. I pray for time and resources to make this happen soon. Maybe camping, fishing, or hunting, but whatever the activity, time to really get to know my kids. Time to talk to them. Time for them to really get to know me too. Refresh us, Lord. Even if our time away is short—only a day and a night. Help me make these short getaways a priority. Just as getting alone with You deepens our relationship, so will my relationship with my kids deepen when I spend time alone with them.

Passing Your Passion on to Your Child

Whatever your hand finds to
do, do it with your might.
ECCLESIASTES 9:10

A dad who shares his passion with his kids will double his pleasure in the activity and will add yet another great bonding experience with his children. But don't forget, too, to find and encourage the passions each child may be developing on his or her own.

Lord, I think it was no accident that Jesus, a carpenter's son, was also a carpenter through the influence of Joseph, the man You appointed to the role of surrogate father here on earth. I'm sure Jesus caught the passion of carpentry from Joseph.

Likewise, God, I have some passionate interests I want to pass on to my kids. Some are mere hobbies, some are lesser interests, but some are passions I believe You've given me. While I pray my kids catch the vision and share my interests, I know You'll put some different passions and interests in their hearts. I pray that just as I want them to share my passions, I will share in the delight of the things they come to love. Help me do that, Lord.

Raising a Pray-er

Lord, teach us to pray.
Luke 11:1

We dads teach our children many things, but few are as important as how to pray. A simple way to start is by helping a child learn The Lord's Prayer. You, Dad, teach your children the familiar prayer and discuss the meaning of each phrase.

Father, as I continue to pray daily for my children, I need to make sure they understand the importance of prayer. Help me teach them that prayer is not about getting things, nor is it merely a bedtime ritual. Prayer is communing with You, our Creator. Prayer is worship. Prayer is listening. Prayer is an anytime/anywhere practice that brings us closer to You. Guide me, Lord, as I teach my kids the importance of prayer and how to pray, and as I encourage them to pray for me.

Bravery

Be watchful, stand firm in the
faith, act like men, be strong.
1 Corinthians 16:13

To be a dad takes bravery. It means leading, often in the face of opposition. It means making prayerful decisions in consultation with your wife. It means praying boldly for what matters to your family. A brave man's soul does not shrink back from responsibility.

God, by Your grace, I am a man of faith and a dad of faith. I'm watchful, firm in the faith, and strong through Your Holy Spirit. I pray that in every opportunity for bravery, I will exhibit courage. I pray I can teach my kids how to be brave and when to be brave—and how to be watchful.

The Giving Father

Every good gift and every perfect gift is from above,
coming down from the Father of lights with whom
there is no variation or shadow due to change.
JAMES 1:17

A father whose moods change with circumstances tends to result in insecure children. Sons and daughters want a dad who does not change on a whim or because of temporary adversity. We dads must be givers, and we should not change like shifting sands.

God, it's important that my kids see me as a man who is stable in my role as a father, not varying with the wind or circumstances. When something is right, I need to defend it. When something is wrong, I need to confront it. I need to be like You in that way, Lord. I need to also be the giver of gifts to my kids—a reflection of You as the giver of perfect gifts.

The Listening Dad

Know this, my beloved brothers: let every person
be quick to hear, slow to speak, slow to anger.
James 1:19

Dads listen to their kids. They hear confessions, prayers, hurts, joys, and sometimes even secrets. At times, they even share their own confessions, prayers, hurts, joys, and secrets with their kids. Dads learn how and when to be transparent with their children. They learn how to listen.

God, I know I need to listen intently, weigh my words, and cool my anger when the kids push my buttons. Help me respond to them the way I wanted my dad to respond to me when I messed up. Bring to mind the times my dad did things right so I can emulate him. Then bring to mind what my dad did wrong so I might avoid the same mistakes. Lord, no matter how my own dad was, please help me be an even better dad.

Staying Away from Evil

Abstain from every form of evil.
1 Thessalonians 5:22

Evil doesn't always shout its presence. Sometimes it presents itself subtly. But a watchful dad sees evil, avoids it himself, and guards his family from it—in its every form.

Lord, in this day and age, it's easy to be tempted by many forms of evil: greed, ambition, sensuality, covetousness, pride, and more. Your Holy Spirit, though, is a great guardian of my soul, enabling me to say no when evil presents itself in its many tempting forms.

For my children, I pray against the easily accessible evil they face. Help me keep temptations at bay and also to know how to teach them to resist temptation through trusting You, prayer, and staying in Your Word.

Keep guard, Lord. We need help in steering clear of evil.

IMAGINATION

O LORD God of Abraham, Isaac, and of Israel, our fathers, keep this for ever in the imagination of the thoughts of the heart of thy people, and prepare their heart unto thee.
1 CHRONICLES 29:18 KJV

Imagination is a gift from God. We're to use it for good, not for evil. Dad, encourage your children to be imaginative, creative, and skilled in seeing what they imagine come to pass. Help them avoid evil imaginations.

Lord, imagination can be good or evil. When surrendered to You, imagination is good, healthy, and creative. For my children, I pray that You will help me lead them in pursuing holy and upright imaginations that can be used for Your glory

Father, I ask you for help with my own sometimes evil imaginations. Help me have a clear, clean mind and use my imaginations in a way that will please You.

Yes, Lord, may my children and I imagine only great things that honor You. I praise you for the wondrous gift of imagining.

Duty and Responsibility

Each of us will give an account of himself to God.
ROMANS 14:12

Being a father is like being given a sum of money to invest for 18 years. At the end of that time, we would expect to see a return on the investment in the form of a reliable man or woman who has landed at adulthood on his or her feet and with his or her faith intact. We dads can look into the faces of the treasure entrusted to us and see great hope, waiting for us to harness all the child's possibilities.

Father, someday I will have to give an account to You of the way I lived—and the way I raised my children. That puts the fear of God in me, Lord. I know there are no do-overs for my kids' childhoods; they get one shot at growing up and I get one shot at growing them up.

I pray that my dad-skills will see my kids grow up spiritually strong and emotionally mature. Help me now, Lord, even today as I move along toward eternity and the day I must stand before You for an accounting.

Studying with Your Child

Do your best to present yourself to God as one
approved, a worker who has no need to be
ashamed, rightly handling the word of truth.
2 Timothy 2:15

When a dad teaches his child from the Bible—even if it's as simple as reading the story of David and Goliath or Jonah and the large fish—the child grasps that this story is important to Dad and thus should be to him or her. Give your child the gift of reading to them from God's Word.

God, as the head of our household, I'm responsible for seeing that the kids know Your Word. If I can give them a strong foundation in the Scriptures, I'll be starting them down the path to a happy life. I pray, then, Lord, for Your wisdom as I impart what I know of the Bible to my children. Though I'm far from a Bible scholar, take what I do know and multiply it, just as Jesus multiplied the loaves and fishes.

Lord, teach me Your Word that I might teach my young ones Your wisdom.

MEMBERS OF ONE ANOTHER

Having put away falsehood, let each one
of you speak the truth with his neighbor,
for we are members one of another.
EPHESIANS 4:25

Think of your family as a small segment of the greater church of God. You are all members of Christ's body and members of your smaller family. As such, you are *members of one another*. That means love and respect for one another. It means unity, even amid the normal family disagreements that arise from time to time. Those spats can never sever the family tie.

Lord, just like Your church, so is our family "members of one another." I need my family and they need me. None of us is a spare tire—we all are essential to our calling as a family.

God, may each member learn to love the other members more fully. May each speak the truth in love to one another and honor one another, and thus honor You as the designer and sustainer of our family.

Combating Racism

*Here there is not Greek and Jew, circumcised
and uncircumcised, barbarian, Scythian,
slave, free; but Christ is all, and in all.*
Colossians 3:11

God's family is made up of all races and ethnic backgrounds. Christian dads teach respect for others by helping their children learn about differing cultures.

Father God, Your kingdom is made up of people from all lands. There is no one preferred race or status—Christ is all and in all.

Help me to instill in my children the rightness of respecting all men and women. Help me to model and then teach my kids to abhor racism in all forms. May they learn to love others, for love is the true mark of a Christian.

A WAITING DAD

I wait for the LORD, my soul
waits, and in his word I hope.
PSALM 130:5

Waiting is hard. But waiting is part of God's means of growing up. We wait for God for many things in life, trusting His timetable over ours. While waiting, we hope in God's Word.

Lord, You know waiting comes hard for me. Like most others, I want answers *now*. I want solutions today, not tomorrow. And yet You instruct me to wait, and while waiting, to hope in Your Word. Thank You that in Your thesaurus "waiting" is a synonym for "learning." As I wait on You and hope in Your Word, I learn the lesson You have appointed for me.

God, I pray you'll show me how to teach my children to wait on You. Kids are even more anxious than their parents. If I can teach them to wait and to hope in Your Word, I will succeed in my job as a father.

Lord, I do wait on you even now. Show me from Your Word how to live rightly. For it's in Your Word that I truly hope.

Teaching Your Child to Be Alone

Fear not, for I am with you; be not dismayed, for I am your God; I will strengthen you, I will help you, I will uphold you with my righteous right hand.

Isaiah 41:10

Someday your children will experience rejection. Perhaps by a friend, or a potential mate, or by a desired employer. Trusting God during times of rejection is crucial. While they're young, teach your children how to handle rejection. Teach them that God is always with them to strengthen them and uphold them with His righteous right hand.

Lord, I know my kids will need to stand alone at times, even in a crowd. They may face ridicule for any differences they have or perhaps even for their faith in You. Help me to teach them to be brave in the face of some of the inevitable rejections they will face in life. I pray they will look to You to uphold them with Your righteous right hand when they need courage. I pray they will never allow themselves to be intimidated into compromising what is right and true. Help them stand strong, Lord. Help me be an example of bravery for them.

TEACHING BEAUTY

He has made everything beautiful in its time.
ECCLESIASTES 3:11

One thing have I asked of the LORD,
that will I seek after:
that I may dwell in the house of the LORD
all the days of my life,
to gaze upon the beauty of the LORD
and to inquire in his temple.
PSALM 27:4

God has revealed Himself through His creation. In the beauty of nature, we see His handiwork. We dads teach our children that though creation is awesome, it's merely a reflection of the Designer who created it. It's God Himself who is truly beautiful. Instill in your children the desire to "gaze upon the beauty of the LORD" someday in eternity.

Father God, I know part of my job as a dad is teaching my kids about You and about this awesome world we live in. Help me slow down along the way and teach them about the beauty of creation. Help me show them that not only is Your creation beautiful, but You, God, are beautiful. You are majestic and glorious. Open our eyes that we may "gaze upon the beauty of the LORD."

A Dad's Trials

Blessed is the man who stays steadfast under trial.
JAMES 1:12

Amid the trials of fatherhood, a mature Christian dad remains steadfast. He won't be shaken by adverse circumstances. Whatever you're facing today, whether at home or on the job, you can remain steadfast. Lean hard on God.

God, you know being a dad has its trials. Sometimes I don't feel up to the challenges. But thank You for the promise that there is a blessing for me if I stay steadfast under parental or any other trials of my faith. Thank You that I can rest in You and wait until the trial passes—as it always does. Help me see Your hidden message in each dad-trial You send my way. I don't want to waste a single one, nor do I want an extra one that brings no growth to me as a father.

When the necessary trials come, Lord, remind me to be patient and trust You—and wait for the blessing at the end.

A Good Attitude

Do all things without grumbling or disputing,
that you may be blameless and innocent,
children of God without blemish in the midst
of a crooked and twisted generation, among
whom you shine as lights in the world.
PHILIPPIANS 2:14-15

Grumbling and disputing seem to be in the genes of our kids. They're no different than we were at that age. A creative dad will try to turn occasions of grumbling into opportunities of praise toward God. We and our kids can be lights in a dark world if we will remain blameless and innocent, and not become grumblers.

Lord, I hate it when the kids question me and grumble about the petty things that bother them. Yet I know I'm that way, too, sometimes. Help me have a long-term vision of my life, and not just focus on daily minutia that blocks my path.

God, we, too, live in the midst of a crooked and twisted generation, and You're calling my family—and all Christians—to shine in the darkness. That light, though, can only come as we reflect *Your* light. May we daily look to You and shine bright as the lighthouses we are in these troubled seas.

LIKE ARROWS IN MY QUIVER

Behold, children are a heritage from the LORD,
the fruit of the womb a reward. Like arrows
in the hand of a warrior are the children of
one's youth. Blessed is the man who fills his
quiver with them! He shall not be put to shame
when he speaks with his enemies in the gate.
PSALM 127:3-5

In our society where some children are considered an inconvenience, and many dads reject their children and turn away from their duty as fathers, it's good to remember that children come from God. They are a blessing. Good dads count not only their own children as a blessing, but all children, including the "fatherless."

Lord, I'm blessed by every arrow You've put in my quiver! Each child is a heritage from You, even though I know I'm only a guardian of children who really belong to You. May I be found faithful—and always thankful—for this assignment You've given me. May I be also mindful of children without a father and their needs.

For each of my "arrows," I now pray for them by name.

Running the Race

Do you not know that in a race all the
runners run, but only one receives the
prize? So run that you may obtain it.
1 Corinthians 9:24

If we dads see life as a long-distance marathon, we know the importance of keeping our nose pointed toward the goal line and running our race with an aim to win. In God's fatherhood marathon there isn't just one winner. Every man who is a faithful dad gets the prize. Run to win, Dad. You can do this.

God, I'm in a race. A dad-race. The goal line is seeing my kids land on their feet as mature adults who are still loving and serving You. I look around at some of the now adult kids of my friends and see that many of them have abandoned their faith. Some are even endangering their lives by flirting with drugs, sexual immorality, and a greedy pursuit of money. Those dads are losing their race—and I don't want to become one of them.

Help me to stand strong in showing my children how to live right and have a successful Christian life. I won't be running this race again, Lord. I'm going to run this race to win the prize.

Providing for Our Children

*If anyone does not provide for his relatives, and
especially for members of his household, he has
denied the faith and is worse than an unbeliever.*

1 Timothy 5:8

Daily we dads give evidence to our faith and to our paternal calling by providing for our children. Even in a two-paycheck family, Dad is ultimately responsible for providing for the household. And from God's point of view, this responsibility is meant to be a blessing to Dad. Men, praise God for His calling on your life as a provider for these people you love.

Among my paternal duties, Lord, is providing for my family. Thank You that through You I'm able to do this. Though You lead me in this duty, I'm the one who carries out the mandate to provide. Through this responsibility, I'm not a denier of the faith, but an affirmer of the faith. I'm acting out the very paternal role You assume for Your children as provider.

God, keep me healthy and faithful in providing for my family, but not with only material needs. As the spiritual leader of the family, I ask you to help me provide spiritually for them as well. Help me keep our eyes turned to You.

Handling Calamity

For the righteous falls seven times and rises again,
but the wicked stumble in times of calamity.
Proverbs 24:16

Every dad falls many more than seven times. It happens. But these same dads get up time and time again and move on. Even during times of family calamity, God strengthens us every time we rise again to get back on the path. If you're facing hard times or family calamity, or if you've just failed in some way, get up, dust yourself off, and get back on the road.

Lord, You know how many times I've fallen—both as a man and as a dad. But with You, there's always the opportunity to get up again and move on. My failures, whether large or small, are all surmountable. With You, there is great forgiveness and mercy.

Lord, may my kids also become great forgivers as I occasionally let them down. Help me order my fatherly steps so that I walk carefully, so that there are fewer stumbles in my future. And when I do stumble, please encourage me as I rise up again to carry on. May I walk in confidence that You will redeem all my failures at the very moment I am back on the road.

FAVOR

A good man obtains favor from the LORD.
PROVERBS 12:2

As "good men" we can expect favor from the Lord. How this happens depends on our present need and the specific circumstance. Many men fail to look to God for favor, and that's to their own loss. God *does* give favor to His children.

I pray today, Lord, that I might be a "good" man, based on my faith in Christ, and obtain favor from You. Favor in all areas of my life, but especially favor as I am a dad to my kids. Teach me to walk in favor daily, believing that in every situation You have gone before me, preparing the way so that it works to my benefit.

In turn, Lord, help me show favor to my kids. May I treat them kindly, demonstrating the favor You have toward Your children.

A Dad's Gentle Rod

*We have had earthly fathers who disciplined us
and we respected them. Shall we not much more
be subject to the Father of spirits and live?*
Hebrews 12:9

Some dads' natural temperaments cause them to react in white-hot anger when they should remain cool and collected. In so doing, the effectiveness of discipline is lost in that tempest of anger. Dads can learn to use the *gentle* rod of correction, like the one God uses on us. Remember to administer discipline as you wish it had been administered to you as a child.

God, some of my friends discipline their children and yet lose the respect of those children. Perhaps they're disciplining out of anger, not love, but the effect is not good and is long lasting. I know You mean my efforts at disciplining my children to be for their benefit, just as Your discipline toward me is to make me a better man. Help me have a firm grasp on the role of discipline. Help me mete out fair punishment for disobedience. May my chastening be just enough to bring about repentance—and never too harsh to bring about bitterness.

As I desire my children to submit to my discipline, so, Lord, do I subject myself to Your gentle rod.

FACING OUR FEARS

I sought the LORD, and he answered me
and delivered me from all my fears.
PSALM 34:4

God saves us from all our fears, dad-related fears included. But it takes seeking the Lord for that to happen. When we seek, He answers and delivers. That's His promise.

Lord God, thank You for delivering me from all my fears—past, present, and future. I now acknowledge my present fear of _____ and trust You to bring deliverance. I pray that I might even become bold through the power of the Holy Spirit in the face of my deepest fears—particularly fears concerning my children, my most valued possessions. I pray for boldness for them, too, Lord. May they slay every source of fear that comes their way. Invest in them, O Lord, through the presence of the Holy Spirit in their young lives.

Father, deliver me from all fears. Be strong in me today.

Our Identity

For where your treasure is, there
will your heart be also.
Luke 12:34

Being a dad isn't just another add-on to our list of identities. Once we become a dad, that role becomes part of our identity DNA. It's who we are. All we do as a dad issues from the dad-heart God has put in us. We mustn't let ourselves forget that most of our priorities are secondary to being a good dad. Our kids are our treasure on earth.

God, sometimes I get my priorities mixed up. My job, my sports hobbies, my puttering around the house—these are just a few of the activities that can temporarily blind me to the needs of my kids to have a father present in their lives. Not just when it's convenient for me, but when it's necessary for them. Rouse me, Lord, from my distracted fog when I need to set aside my planned day and make time for the kids.

Help me remember that You do that, Father. You are there for me 24/7, demonstrating that I'm a priority with You. May I do the same for my children.

Laboring in Prayer

Pray without ceasing.
1 Thessalonians 5:17

Dads pray for their kids—without ceasing. There's always a need or request to be made on behalf of our kids. God delights in our ceaseless prayers and He delights to answer.

Lord, as a dad, I know You call me to be the chief intercessor for my children. Daily I lift them before You for Your blessing on them and Your wisdom for me. I pray for them without ceasing. Even as I go about my day, my thoughts are not far from them. Their good is my constant prayer.

As my children are small, then adolescents, and eventually adults, I will continue to be their intercessor, believing that You—a father yourself—hear my prayers and answer them. What more important duty do I have as a dad than to diligently pray for my kids without ceasing, entrusting them to You?

Serving the God Who Restores

Restore to me the joy of your salvation, and
uphold me with a willing spirit.
Psalm 51:12

With God, it's never too late to start fresh. In fact, most of us need the joy of our salvation restored practically daily. Salvation for a Christian is, indeed, a cause for great joy. Reflect on how great your salvation is and how the joy of that salvation affects your fathering duties.

Lord, some days I need a fresh sense of Your presence in my life. Today is one of those days. I pray You will restore the joy of my salvation. Rekindle the flame of faith in my heart. Increase my love for You…and for my kids. I pray for a renewed and deepened love for the children You've given me. I ask You to uphold me as a dad and give me the willing spirit to be all my kids need me to be.

TRUSTING IN GOD'S SOVEREIGNTY

*The heart of man plans his way, but
the LORD establishes his steps.*
PROVERBS 16:9

Though God is never surprised, sometimes we are. And yet God is the one at work in us every day. He watches over us with great care, and His sovereignty is our ally in life as dads. Since nothing surprises God, nothing should shake us when it happens. God is always in control, no matter what.

Lord, sometimes Your plans throw me for a loop. I think I know what's up, and then all of a sudden something happens that confuses me. I know You are sovereign and You do all things in accordance with Your divine plan, but when these unexpected changes happen in my family, I ask, "How, Lord, will You work this out?" The answer to what puzzles me is always to wait, watch, and trust.

Your sovereignty isn't my enemy; it's my friend. Lord, I therefore trust You to work out for my good—and the good of my kids—every seeming interruption to my own plans. I give You charge of my life. Every bit of it.

Home Is Where Dad Is

He who dwells in the shelter of the Most High
will abide in the shadow of the Almighty. I
*will say to the L*ord, *"My refuge and my*
fortress, my God, in whom I trust."
P*salm* 91:1-2

A good dad can help define what home is. The sheltering aspect of a strong father builds security in a child. You don't have to be Superman to be a refuge and fortress for your kids. You just have to be there and love them.

Father, in my calling to be a dad, You've also called me to be, like You, a refuge and fortress for my kids. I'm their earthly protector. Our home is a shelter from the storms of the world. Gird me to be that strong protector of my family. I pray for strength that I sometimes don't have—but You do. I pray, too, specifically for our home. I pray our kids will know that home means security, safety, and refuge, just as You, O Lord, are my refuge and fortress.

PRACTICE MAKES PERFECT

*What you have learned and received and
heard and seen in me—practice these things,
and the God of peace will be with you.*
PHILIPPIANS 4:9

It should come as no surprise that, as with most everything else in life, practice makes perfect when it comes
to fatherhood. Today you're a better father than you
were a year ago. A year from now, you'll be a better
father than you are now. Practice dad-hood daily, and
the God of peace will watch over you.

Practice makes perfect, Lord. As a dad, I have learned
much from how I was parented, how I see other dads
act, and what Your Word teaches. I see that being a
dad is really an on-the-job training endeavor, so I learn
as I go. I pray You'll continue to design specific situations that help me learn how to be a great dad. Daily I
try to practice these things, and I pray that Your peace
will be with me and prevail in our home.

DAD AT CHURCH

*Let us consider how to stir up one another to love
and good works, not neglecting to meet together, as
is the habit of some, but encouraging one another,
and all the more as you see the Day drawing near.*
HEBREWS 10:24-26

A good church is vital to the health of a Christian
family. Not only do we grow by what we learn
at church, we enjoy worshiping God together, and we
become bonded with other families that share our values. Make your church a matter of regular prayer. Help
your kids develop a love for their church family.

Lord, You love Your church, the bride of Christ. Help me
to love the church with the same passion—and then to
pass that passion on to my kids. I don't want my children to think of church as boring or unnecessary. I want
them to find meaning as they fellowship with other
believers. I want that for myself too. Help us as a family
to love and participate with the others with whom we
regularly gather to worship You. Thank You for a good
church fellowship.

An Affectionate Dad

Love one another with brotherly affection.
ROMANS 12:10

Love without affection is like a glove without a hand. Show your children affection in the ways they desire. Not all kids receive affection the same way. Let your child decide how they want you to show affection. Find out their "love language" by reading the popular book *The 5 Love Languages of Children* by Gary Chapman and Ross Campbell.

Lord, I know some dads have a hard time showing affection to their kids. Yet all kids need a good measure of fatherly affection. I sure did when I was a boy. And now that I'm a dad, I want to be an affectionate father to my children. When I show them affection, it's a reminder that my love means security for them—and they crave security from their dad.

Today, Lord, may I not become too busy to find a way to show affection to my kids. And, Lord, please let me never forget the affection You have for me.

GOD, THE PERFECT FATHER

You therefore must be perfect, as your
heavenly Father is perfect.
MATTHEW 5:48

Perfection as a dad is a lofty goal. We are already "perfect" in our standing with God through Christ. We are justified from all our sin. Utterly forgiven. But translating a perfect standing before God into perfect standing as a dad in the eyes of our children is not easily achieved. And yet, that's our goal. We want to be perfect dads within the capabilities and talents God has given us. And this we can do.

Lord, when I look in Your Word, I see as in a mirror the kind of dad You want me to be. My kids may never see me as perfect—I sure didn't see my dad that way—but I want them to know that I use the dad-talents You've given me to the best of my ability. I know I can and will be a great dad as I allow You to shape my life as a father. In myself, I miss the mark by a long shot, so Lord, help me fix my aim closer to the bull's-eye. Help move me closer to perfect-dad status.

BOLD FAITH

We have boldness and access with confidence
through our faith in [Christ].
EPHESIANS 3:12

Dads never need be shy about praying boldly for their children. The bolder the prayer, the more God likes it. Boldness means we believe God will answer.

Father, it's with boldness and confidence that I pray for my children. You have given them to me and have assigned me the role of being their father. Therefore, I pray boldly for Your blessing on their young lives. Create a heart in them that hungers for You. Keep them from danger and dangerous people. May they have a holy hatred for the sin that so easily besets us. Call them, Lord, not just into Your kingdom, but into Your service. Give them a mission in this life designed just for them.

Thank You, Father, for hearing my bold prayer.

Safety from the Evil One

*The Lord is faithful. He will establish you
and guard you against the evil one.*
2 Thessalonians 3:3

Christian families are under attack from the Evil One—perhaps especially dads. For protection, our reliance is on God to guard us. This assurance, like every other aspect of the Christian life, comes by faith. Have faith that God is protecting you. Trust Him.

Father, I know the Enemy tries his best to attack my family—particularly the kids. I thank You for the promise to establish our family and to guard us against the Evil One, no matter his wicked schemes. Thank You that we are prepared to stand against his attacks and come out victorious. I pray You will keep the guard up around our home. Protect us from unexpected attempts on my family's security and happiness. Guard us in danger. Keep us healthy, both physically and spiritually. Thank You for Your faithfulness!

Overcoming Worry

Casting all your anxieties on [God],
because he cares for you.
1 Peter 5:7

Anxiety comes to everyone at some time or another. A dad's anxieties may center around his children, his marriage, his job, finances, health, or any number of other things. But God tells us to cast *all* our anxieties on Him. Why? Because He cares for us. Today, you can do that. You can, right now, cast all your worries and concerns on Him, knowing He cares enough for you to take them on Himself.

God of all peace, being a dad has some anxieties attached to it. But You care for me and You know my anxieties. You know when I feel incompetent and You know when I'm the picture of confidence. In those times of anxiety, I cast them all on You. I trust You to work out the cause of my fears in Your own perfect way. I pray my anxieties will never affect my children.

A Man of Peace

May the Lord of peace himself give you
peace at all times in every way.
2 Thessalonians 3:16

Sometimes the home is peaceful and, if your family is like most, sometimes there's a tornado loose in the house. God is the Lord of peace for us. He brings peace into every life and every home that invites His peace to reside there. May your home accept the Lord of peace, and may He grant you peace at all times and in every way.

God, You are the Lord of peace and You give me peace at all times and in every way. I especially pray that Your peace will guide me in my role as a dad. I pray my kids will see the peace You give and know that it doesn't come naturally to me, but comes supernaturally from You.

May Your peace prevail in my home and heart.

GIVER OF GIFTS

If you then, who are evil, know how to
give good gifts to your children, how much
more will your Father who is in heaven
give good things to those who ask him!

MATTHEW 7:11

God gives good gifts to His children. But when does He do that? When we ask. May God today bring good to you as you ask Him to be your giver of gifts. Then, give back to Him your praise and gratitude.

Lord, my kids look to me to be their provider, just as I look to You to provide for me. Help me in this role as I try to be generous, but also wise. Help me know how to give what they *need* in addition to what they want.

And thank You for being so generous toward me, God. I see Your gifts to me daily and I appreciate every one. Thank You for giving when I ask. Thank You for being the perfect dad.

Overcoming Dad Burnout

*Jesus said to them, "Truly, truly, I say to you, the
Son can do nothing of his own accord, but only
what he sees the Father doing. For whatever
the Father does, that the Son does likewise."*

John 5:19

Jesus didn't do everything He could do; He did *only* what He saw the Father doing. Sometimes He said an inner "no" to what God was not leading Him to do. Likewise, many fathers take on too much, including responsibilities that aren't really theirs. If that's you, pray about how to tactfully say no to future requests and how to delegate projects that aren't really yours to manage. That will relieve you from much stress and have a positive effect on your role as a father.

Lord, sometimes I take on too much. Then when I get burned out, I tend to take it out on the family, either by shortchanging them on my time or by becoming quick-tempered, easily angered. Help me step back and reassess my priorities. If I need to let some things go, help me make that decision and follow through. In all of this feeling of burnout, I pray You'll give me a fresh sense of Your Spirit. Help me do what You want me to do in my life, not what I merely think I should be doing.

The Gift of a Sober Dad

Do not get drunk with wine, for that is
debauchery, but be filled with the Spirit.
Ephesians 5:18

Addictions among dads is epidemic. Some of those addictions are to drugs or alcohol—and at a time when more than ever we need sober and straight-thinking fathers to bring up the next generation. Your kids need a sober dad. Not only sobriety from alcohol and drugs, but sobriety from any addiction that interferes with your family life. Take stock of yourself. Have you been unwilling to admit to an addiction? Get help. Start with God and go from there. Be filled with God's Spirit.

God, I pray You'll keep me a sober man. I pray my kids will never see me under the influence of drugs or alcohol, but only under the influence of Your Holy Spirit. I know my kids—like all kids—are likely to copy any addictions they see in Dad, so for their sake as well as mine, I pray for a life of sobriety, being filled only by Your Spirit.

I also pray for my kids as they're exposed to various temptations to alcohol or drugs in our present culture. May Your Spirit satisfy them with Your inner presence.

Lord, I praise You for Your Spirit within. You are the One who satisfies the longing soul.

GOD'S UNSEEN WORK
IN OUR CHILDREN

Trust in the Lord with all your heart, and
do not lean on your own understanding.
PROVERBS 3:5

Dads can't know everything about their kids. Much goes on in the interior life of a child that is never seen by either parent. That's when Dad and Mom must not lean on their own understanding of their child, but trust him or her to God with all their heart.

God, when it gets right down to it, sometimes I don't know the right dad-decision to make. Sometimes I guess wrong. When I do, I pray You'll help me make things right with my child. I pray that as I move ahead in fatherhood, I won't be tempted to lean on my own faulty understanding but will rely on You and Your wisdom. I pray that You'll be working 24/7 in the lives of my children. I pray Your unseen hand will sculpt their interior lives in ways I could never do.

Yes, Lord, I trust You with my kids. Do a work in their hearts that only You can do.

God Leads Dads

He tends his flock like a shepherd:
He gathers the lambs in his arms
and carries them close to his heart;
he gently leads those that have young.

Isaiah 40:11 niv

Shepherds have one priority: their sheep. They must see that the sheep are in good pasture, that they have water, and that they're protected. The Lord is our Good Shepherd, but we are an undershepherd to our children.

Lord, my Good Shepherd, thank You for tending to me with such care. You watch over me and keep me from going off on my own. You carry me close to Your heart and You gently lead me as I tend to my young. I would not be a father had You not given me my children, and now as a father, I depend on You to lead me as a good dad—as a good shepherd to the lambs You've given me. I thank You for each of them. May I be the dad they need in every respect.

NO PLAYING FAVORITES

God shows no partiality.
ROMANS 2:11

Kids can sense when Dad shows partiality toward a sibling. You may feel closer—more bonded—to one of your children than to the others, but that doesn't mean you don't love them all, and your actions must bear that out. Any differentiation in your feelings must be your secret. Your children should each feel certain, through your active love, that you care for them just as much as you care for their sisters and brothers.

God, I'm reminded that You love all Your children—without measure. Help me to love my kids equally and help me let them know I do not show partiality toward one over another. You have given me the capacity to love each of my children with 100 percent of my love. If one of my children is feeling less loved over a sibling, please allow me to pick up on that and deal with it. If the problem is with me—if I *am* showing partiality—help me make it right with the child whom I have offended.

Thank You for not favoring others of Your children, Lord, but for loving me with 100 percent of Your love.

Showing Compassion

As a father shows compassion to his children, so the
Lord shows compassion to those who fear him.
Psalm 103:13

It's natural for a dad to be compassionate toward his children. When he is doing so, he is displaying an attribute of God. If you have a child who needs your compassion today, don't withhold it. Offer it freely.

God, You model what compassion for children looks like in Your dealings with me. I'm a blessed man and I know it. I don't deserve the gifts You've given me, especially my family. It's only because of Your compassion that I have what I have. Left to myself, I'd be far from where I am now.

Now, God, may I show fatherly compassion to my own children. Compassion that springs from a true father-heart, just as Your Father-heart is compassionate toward me.

A Good Man

*A good man leaves an inheritance to
his children's children, but the sinner's
wealth is laid up for the righteous.*
PROVERBS 13:22

Not all inheritances are monetary. You can begin now gathering up the values and traits you want to leave behind in your children. If you impart to them goodness, faith, and love, they will go further on that inheritance than on a financial legacy. History is replete with young heirs of great fortunes whose lives were ruined because of a legacy of money.

God, I want to be a good man—and a good dad. But when I think of an inheritance I can leave to my children, I think first of their inheritance of faith. If I can leave behind the legacy of a man who loved and served God well, that is a precious inheritance worth more than any earthly heirloom.

As I increase in faith, as I move along as a dad, I pray for interest to be gathered on this inheritance I leave my children. Compound the interest, Lord. May the gold of my faith be multiplied many times before I leave my children behind.

And God, I praise You for my own inheritance, won for me by Christ, my Lord. Thank You.

NATURE: GOD'S SCHOOLHOUSE

*On the glorious splendor of your majesty, and
on your wondrous works, I will meditate.*
PSALM 145:5

Nature is a terrific teacher. A wise dad can make a fun and valuable lesson from a hike through the woods or an overnight campout. Even a walk out in the backyard on a starry night will declare the wonder of God. Teach your children to look for God's handiwork in nature.

Father God, thank You for nature. Each morning I look outside and see the works of creation that scream aloud of Your greatness. Your wondrous works declare Your majesty. You alone are worthy of praise. As I teach my kids about Your creation, I pray You'll give me insight into the life lessons to be found in nature. Such lessons are there every day, if I'll only take time to observe them. Today show me a fresh revelation about You from nature that I can share with my children.

I give You glory, Lord, for all I see around me. It's absolutely stunning!

Praying Out Loud

I cry aloud to God…and he will hear me.
Psalm 77:1

Time usually dictates that we pray quietly to ourselves, perhaps even thinking our prayers. That's fine, but when we can pray aloud in a normal tone of voice, it somehow seems more real to us. Today, find a quiet time when you can pray aloud for each of your kids. Maybe on your lunch hour, go sit in the car and offer a prayer. God hears either way, but there's power in voiced prayers.

O Lord, You hear my every prayer! You're there even when I doubt. You always come through in the way that's best for me. Today I pray to You with my voice. I call on You to strengthen me, uphold me, guide me, and enable me to be a great dad. I know it starts with a heart that beats with the same fatherly passion as Yours.

Give me that heart. Give me the pure paternal love for my kids that You have toward me. For this I pray aloud today. Grant it, Lord.

God as Our Source

My God will supply every need of yours
according to his riches in glory in Christ Jesus.
PHILIPPIANS 4:19

Dads whose jobs are lost because of downsizing, but who don't look to God as their source, may soon find themselves in a downward spiral spiritually. God supplies our needs according to His riches in glory, not according to our employer's bank account. Trust God to be your supplier today and always, no matter what happens with your job.

God, it's easy for me to attribute the supplying of my needs to my paycheck or my hard work, but You are my supplier for all "riches." You are responsible for my source of income and all my family's provision. I trust in You for all our needs. You give abundance, Lord, and entrust me with much. Help me be a better steward of the goods You bestow on me. Make me mindful of the needs of others so I can be a channel You use to supply their needs.

Lord, I thank You for all Your past provision, I honor You for Your present provision, and I look to You for all our future needs.

IMITATE GOOD

Beloved, do not imitate evil but imitate good.
3 John 1:11

Kids are great imitators. They like to walk in Dad's footsteps…even his shoes sometimes. Likewise, we want to imitate our heavenly Father. We want to imitate good and we want our kids to imitate us imitating good. Make good actions your everyday goal.

Thank You, Lord, that You've not called me just to be a dad, but to be a *good* dad. Keep my feet from evil and—just as important—keep my eyes from evil. I pray Your Holy Spirit will prick my conscience when I linger too long watching a movie that is intrinsically evil or when I happen on an internet image or magazine photo that pulls my attention away from "good."

God, I know that when I imitate good, I'm imitating You, for You are always good. Because I want my kids to be good adults, I pray You'll remind our entire family that we should always be imitators of good and avoid the evil attractions and deeds that rob us of the abundant life You have for us.

SECRETS CAN DESTROY US

*You have set our iniquities before you, our
secret sins in the light of your presence.*
PSALM 90:8

Men who harbor secrets—especially secret sins—
are walking on thin ice. If they're not careful,
the ice may break and plunge them into a cold darkness. Dads, don't have secrets that wear away your conscience. Get rid of them. Live in such a way that your
every thought and action could be made public without embarrassment.

O God, if my secret sins were known by others, I'd not
be able to stand. You know those sins, Lord. You know
even the ones I only entertain in my imagination, but
never act on. And, yes, You know the ones I act on.

Father God, I put those sins before You and ask
for cleansing and deliverance. I pray for a pure heart
toward You and toward my family. Thank You for the
complete forgiveness I have in Christ. Help me to live
out that forgiveness and the deliverance from my
secret sins. I cast them all on You, Lord, and receive
from You the power to live in victory over the temptations of my flesh.

Our True Work

Commit your work to the LORD, and
your plans will be established.
PROVERBS 16:3

Many busy men get caught up in a work that may not be their true work. It may even be a good work, but remember the old saying that "the good is the enemy of the best." What is your best and true work? Set that at the forefront of your mind today and every day. Let your true work of fatherhood be the work you commit to the Lord.

Lord, what is my true work here on earth? No, it's not my job. I get that. I know my true work is depositing truth in the lives of my children. It's giving them the foundation they need for a successful life. My true work is loving my kids in such a way that they know the truth without a single doubt.

Father, keep me clear on the important job I have of parenting my kids. I commit this true work to You, God. Establish my life as a good father. Bless my kids as I lead them into truth.

STAGES OF FATHERHOOD

For everything there is a season, and a
time for every matter under heaven.
ECCLESIASTES 3:1

Wherever you are now, today, in your fatherhood journey, it will soon pass and you will enter a new phase with your children. That's normal and right. Sometimes the transitions unfold so slowly that we don't really notice them. Dads, whatever stage you're in right now, treasure it while you have it. This day and year is a gift from God. Someday, much too quickly, you will look back with fondness at where you are today. Take time to enjoy this stage. Don't be so eager for the next stage. It will come soon enough.

Father, You see where I am now in my role as a dad. You see the stages of fatherhood behind me and before me. Help me to be a great dad during this present stage, knowing it will soon change as the kids grow up. May I easily discern the differences in each stage of fathering and act accordingly, knowing what worked two years ago may not work now. Allow me to fully see each of my children where they are *now* and to see what their needs are *now*. Awaken me, Lord, as each new stage approaches. Prepare me for the necessary changes.

WALKING IN THE TRUTH

I have no greater joy than to hear that my
children are walking in the truth.
3 JOHN 1:4

The apostle John had no greater joy than knowing his "children" were walking in the truth. That's our goal as dads too. You will find no greater joy than seeing your kids grasp the truth and walk in it.

Father, Your Word is truth. To walk in truth is to walk in step with Your Word. I pray that not only will I be diligent about walking in the truth, but that I will teach my children how to walk in the truth. I pray they will take naturally to the Word, as a duck takes to water. Help me show them the practical importance of knowing Your Word and living it out in daily life. Bring me, Lord, the true joy that comes from obedience to Your Word—both for me as a father and for my children.

KINDNESS

*Be kind to one another, tenderhearted, forgiving
one another, as God in Christ forgave you.*
EPHESIANS 4:32

Learn to forget your child's sins as soon as they're confessed and dealt with. Don't bring up remembrances of past sins or even childish mistakes. God doesn't do that with you…and aren't you glad?

Lord, how kind You are to me. Tenderhearted and forgiving. You have forgiven my many sins and You rejoice in me as Your son.

When my kids think of me years from now, I want them to think of me as a kind, tenderhearted, and forgiving dad. It seems almost every day you arrange situations that will allow me to model these qualities. Help me remember that every difficult circumstance is designed by You to reveal what I'm made of. May only tenderness be revealed today.

SACRIFICE

*By this we know love, that he laid
down his life for us, and we ought to
lay down our lives for the brothers.*
1 JOHN 3:16

Being a dad is a sacrificial calling. You have to give up some of your time, money, energy, and emotion to pour out your life for your kids. But Jesus poured out His life for us, and we greatly benefit from His sacrifice. Your kids will also benefit from your sacrifice. And you will receive more from sacrificial living than living for yourself. Living for yourself gets old real fast.

God, it's hard to imagine the depth of love that will sacrifice life and limb for another person. Truly, such a person has already died to the kind of self-love that puts personal interests first. You demonstrated that kind of love on the cross, and now we who are Christians are to follow in the steps of Jesus and lay down our lives for our brothers. Sometimes literally, sometimes by simply denying our own wants in favor of our brothers and sisters. Or our children.

Lord, help me lay down my life for my kids. Help me lay aside my golf game, favorite TV show, or night out with the guys to be present with my family.

No Corrupt Talk

Let no corrupting talk come out of your mouths,
but only such as is good for building up, as fits the
occasion, that it may give grace to those who hear.
EPHESIANS 4:29

Dads, we need to watch what comes out of our mouths. Our job is to build up our kids, not tear them down. Find something affirming to say to each of your children tonight. Make it a habit.

Lord, when I read Your Word, I'm amazed at all the wonderful things You say about me and my new identity in You. I'm astonished at all the promises You make for me. I love the many affirmations of my value and Your love for me. You're constantly building me up as I read Your Word, believing what it says about me.

Father, I pray that I may likewise affirm my kids. Help me build them up with words of grace—not corrupt talk that only brings them down. Put a guard before my mouth so that I leave unsaid any corrupt words that could harm or undermine my children's sense of worth.

Burden Bearing

Bear one another's burdens, and
so fulfill the law of Christ.
GALATIANS 6:2

All dads have burdens every so often. Sometimes lesser burdens, sometimes weightier ones. Such burdens are made lighter when the load is shared. Do you know other fathers at church who will share your burdens as you share theirs? Older fathers, especially, are fountains of wisdom. Seek them out when you need help with a troublesome matter. God will send the right person.

God, being a dad does bring a special set of both joys and burdens. Thank You that You have given me men in my church who are also dads and who can bear my burdens as I bear theirs. It's good for us to share our experiences and compare fathering tips. It's good just to have fellowship with like-minded men.

Today, You know my burdens for my children. I pray You will also bear the load with me, just as my brothers have done. Thank You, Lord, that You are the great burden bearer for Your people.

Making God Laugh

Many are the plans in the mind of a man, but
it is the purpose of the LORD that will stand.
PROVERBS 19:21

Dads, make sure your plans are in line with the purposes of God. Confirm your plans by prayer, by seeing how they line up with God's Word, by the advice of trusted men you know (and your wife), and open doors (favorable circumstances). Wise dads don't embark on elaborate schemes without good counsel.

Lord, I remember that old joke that says if you want to make God laugh, tell Him your plans. And yes, Lord, I do have plans and ideas about how things should go. But because I know and trust You, I defer to Your purposes. Your plans will stand while mine will inevitably crumble under the unfolding of daily life. Help me align every aspect of my life with Your purposes and adjust my own plans so they are merely an implementation of Your will.

INSTILLING LOVE OF COUNTRY

Honor everyone. Love the brotherhood.
Fear God. Honor the emperor.
1 PETER 2:17

Dads, make sure your kids know the history of America, particularly the influence of the Bible in the founding of our country. Teach them that those values are still crucial to keeping freedom alive. Teach them to pray for America and its leaders.

Lord, what a blessing to live in this great nation where I'm free to worship You and free to teach my children to honor You. As a dad, I am teaching my kids to honor others, no matter what their ethnicity or background. I'm teaching them to love their Christian brothers and sisters. Perhaps even more, I'm teaching them to fear You—knowing the fear of the Lord is still the beginning of wisdom.

Finally, I'm teaching them to respect those in authority. I'm joining them in praying for our leaders and teaching them to pray good men and women into positions of authority. God, I pray You will continue to bless my country and keep it strong. Keep it free.

The Day of Salvation

Believe in the Lord Jesus, and you will
be saved, you and your household.
Acts 16:31

In several places in the Bible, we see God saving entire households, not just individuals. Believe that God wants all the members of your family to come to know Him. Teach your children the necessity of having their own relationship with Christ. Pray for them and with them.

Father, as I read my Bible, I notice how often Your intention is to save not just individuals, but also households. Noah's entire family was saved from destruction. In the Passover, the blood of the lamb was sufficient for the entire family to be spared. Rahab was not saved alone through her obedience, but also her family. In the book of Acts, several households are reported as saved.

Lord, for my own family, I believe and claim household salvation. I trust You for the salvation of each family member as they trust in Christ. I pray not only for my present family, but for my future descendants. May our family be part of an ongoing legacy of believers in Christ who dedicate their lives to You.

GOD'S MASTERPIECE

We are God's masterpiece.
EPHESIANS 2:10 NLT

God, the ultimate artist, as seen by His handiwork in nature, can also be observed by looking in the mirror and beholding His masterpiece in progress. He began a good work in you and He will finish it. Every day brings another stroke of His brush and the picture becomes clearer. Dad, rejoice at what God's doing in you; even if you don't see it, God does.

God, my children are Your masterpieces in progress. With deft strokes of Your brush, You paint the lines that are forming them. With divine hands, You sculpt their bodies. With Your Spirit, You implant a desire for You in their hearts.

As you have done with them, so do with me, Lord. For I, too, am Your child—another of Your masterpieces in progress.

You Are the Father of God's Special Child

I praise you, for I am fearfully and wonderfully made.
Wonderful are your works; my soul knows it very well.
My frame was not hidden from you, when I was being
made in secret, intricately woven in the depths of the
earth. Your eyes saw my unformed substance; in your
book were written, every one of them, the days that were
formed for me, when as yet there was none of them.
Psalm 139:13-16

Just as every child is special to God, so is every dad. You and your child are custom-made for each other. He or she has lessons to learn from you, and you have lessons to learn from your child. Today, Dad, rejoice in the specialness of your children to God. And in your own specialness too.

Wow, Lord. Your way of bringing new children into the world is amazing. Babies truly are fearfully and wonderfully made, and every child is a God-designed child with a God-designed purpose.

I pray You'll never let me forget that I'm the father of Your very special children. Give me grace and give my children grace as we grow together. And never let me forget that I'm Your special child too.

A Dad's Dark Night of the Soul

Weeping may stay for the night, but
rejoicing comes in the morning.
PSALM 30:5 NIV

Most dads endure at least one dark night of the soul, but they must never endure it alone. God will often send others to stand by them. Or perhaps, because they have had such an experience, send them to stand by another dad who's enduring a dark night.

If others are not with you during dark nights of the soul, certainly God walks with you. Never fear during those dark nights. Rejoicing comes in the morning.

Dear God, fatherhood sure has its ups and downs. I love the ups, but the downs tear at my soul. They hurt. Surely You know that more than I do. It was a dark night of the soul when Your Son was crucified at the hands of men You Yourself created. Thank You, Lord, that Your dark night of the soul brought rejoicing on the morning of resurrection.

Lord, I long for this present dark night to end soon. Bring about resurrection, redemption, resolution. Give me strength to hang on until I can once again rejoice in the morning.

FATHERS: ONE OF SATAN'S PRIME TARGETS

Be sober-minded; be watchful. Your adversary the devil prowls around like a roaring lion, seeking someone to devour.
1 PETER 5:8

Every dad needs to develop his built-in trouble detector. Our children's adversary, the devil, sneaks in when we're not observant. Once he gets a toehold, he always wants more. The best time to stop the attack is at the very beginning, by being watchful. Pray often for protection over your children against the adversary's attacks.

Father, I know Satan wants me to fail as a dad. He has his eyes on my kids, targeting them for harm. If possible, he'd like to use me as a means to that end. But You, Lord, the Lion of Judah, are my protector from this ravenous lion on the prowl. Keep me watchful of his tactics to undermine my role as a father and devour my family. Remind me that I have authority over the Enemy and that greater is He that is in me than he that is in the world.

When You Have to Say No

*Going a little farther [Jesus] fell on his
face and prayed, saying, "My Father, if
it be possible, let this cup pass from me;
nevertheless, not as I will, but as you will."*

Matthew 26:39

Jesus prayed for His Father to let the cup of suffering pass from Him. But it was not to be. God's plan for our redemption necessitated the agony of the cross. Saying no to our kids when we know no is the right answer is the right thing to do, no matter how much they plead with us to reverse our decision. Make sure you say yes often, but never be sorry for a well-thought-out no.

Lord, I remember how Jesus prayed to You, His Father, asking if the cup awaiting Him might be passed over. But You had to say no so Scripture might be fulfilled and that Christ might die for our sins. It was Your will to not grant a yes to this prayer from Your beloved Son.

Sometimes my kids beg me for something I truly want them to have, but I have to say no because I realize it's not the best for them. Lord, I pray You will give me discernment concerning my yeses and nos. And I even pray for more yeses and fewer nos. But most of all, I pray, "Not as I will, but as You will" in all I decide for my kids.

Abba, Father!

Because you are sons, God has sent the Spirit of his Son into our hearts, crying, "Abba! Father!"
GALATIANS 4:6

What greater delight does a dad have than when his kids run into his arms when he arrives home from work or after a business trip? God expresses that same delight when we have the "Abba! Father!" attitude His Holy Spirit creates in us. Take joy today in knowing God as your "daddy."

Lord, I love it when the kids greet me with "Daddy!" when I walk in the door. Sometimes they rush into my arms for hugs and kisses. I'm delighted that they love to see me and be held by me. There's something about that feeling that carries over into my relationship with You. No, I don't run into Your arms, but I still think of You with joy as my heavenly Father. At times, I do want to cry out, "Abba! Father!' at how good You are to me. You have made me Your son. You have sent Your Spirit into my heart, enabling my happy cry. Lord, may it be so today—and every day. You are my Abba Father.

Dad as Encourager

Fathers, do not provoke your children,
lest they become discouraged.
Colossians 3:21

Good dads need encouragement. They also need to be encouragers, not provokers, of the family. Mom and the kids need to hear Dad urge them on in their endeavors. They especially need encouragement after a failure or after they've blown it in some way.

Make sure each family member knows you're a charter member of their fan club.

Lord, sometimes I let off a little steam when my kids blow it. I'm sure the result is that I provoke them, and perhaps, not realizing it, I'm also discouraging them.

Help me avoid provoking my children. I pray You'll instead show me ways to encourage them and lift them up, even when they disappoint me. Help me build up my kids by complimenting them on a job well done and showing them how to improve when they're not doing their best. And when they blow it, Lord, help me keep calm and resolve the situation peacefully.

DAD AS PRAYER WARRIOR

We do not wrestle against flesh and blood, but
against the rulers, against the authorities, against
the cosmic powers over this present darkness, against
the spiritual forces of evil in the heavenly places.
EPHESIANS 6:12

Nothing brings us to our knees faster than trouble. Sometimes that trouble is an attack on our family from the Enemy. At such times, dads become warriors—prayer warriors. We have great authority in providing prayer protection for our families.

God, it's no surprise the Enemy has designs on my children. Spiritual forces of evil always seek to destroy innocence. That was true even of Jesus, who was tempted by the devil. Surely if Your Son was the target of Satan, so, too, are my children.

As my kids' dad, You've instilled in me a paternal instinct to protect them. You've empowered me to pray over each child, knowing that You back up my prayers to shut down Satan's attacks on them.

Father, knowing the Enemy works best under the cover of darkness, make me aware of any new designs on my children and direct me to pray with divine authority against those demonic schemes. Lord, the Enemy cannot have my children.

A Dad Who Thanks God, No Matter What

*Giving thanks always and for everything to God
the Father in the name of our Lord Jesus Christ.*
EPHESIANS 5:20

A dad's time of prayer should always include thanksgiving. We have so much to thank God for. Take time now to praise Him for at least five specific blessings He's brought into your life.

Today, Lord, I have much to be thankful for. I don't feel that way every day, though I know I should. Thankfulness is always in order, no matter what.

Each day brings a fresh set of dad-related circumstances, and sometimes they throw me off balance. On those days, help me to remember to give thanks always, no matter what. You are always in control and always good.

God, here are five of the many things for which I praise and thank You.

1. _____
2. _____
3. _____
4. _____
5. _____

A House Must Be a Home

By wisdom a house is built, and by understanding
it is established; by knowledge the rooms are
filled with all precious and pleasant riches.
PROVERBS 24:3-4

A wise dad knows that beyond his many chores around the house and yard, there's also the duty of turning the house into a home—with Mom's help, of course. Your house will hold memories for your children. Make those memories good ones. Help the kids personalize their rooms. Ask them to help you decide where to plant that new tree. Create a special play space where you wrestle on the floor with them. Don't forget a place where you pray as a family.

Lord, when I consider our home, I want to think of it as the place where You bring blessing. I want our home to be a shelter of peace, love, and security.

Help me build that kind of home. Help me with the wisdom, understanding, and knowledge that will furnish our rooms with precious and pleasant riches. O God, I invite You to be the Lord of our home.

Teaching Self-Worth

*Even the hairs of your head are all numbered. Fear
not; you are of more value than many sparrows.*
Luke 12:7

No child in a Christian family should doubt his or her worth or suffer from poor self-esteem. They are all created in God's image and He measures their every breath, numbers the hairs on their head, and counts them as more valuable than many sparrows. Kids must learn early of their value in God's eyes—and in yours, Dad.

I praise You, Lord. Thank You for loving me and my family. Thank You for providing for us every day. Thank You that each one of us in the family is unique and imbued with the talents you've placed in us. You have even numbered the hairs on all our heads. Our value to You is more than that of many sparrows. I pray you will help me instill in my children a sense of their self-worth, having been created by You in Your image. Help me give them the confidence that comes from being loved and cared for by You. I pray for our entire household, that we both individually and as a family will grasp the depth of Your love for us.

STEWARDING THE ENVIRONMENT

*The LORD God took the man and put him in
the garden of Eden to work it and keep it.*
GENESIS 2:15

Great dads teach their sons and daughters to be good stewards of all that God has given them, including the environment. Help your children understand what it means to be a "steward," and ask them for suggestions for how you as a family can take better care of what God's given you.

Father, I thank You for this earth. I thank You for all the resources we have: land to produce food, air to breathe, water to drink, mountains to climb, oceans and lakes to swim in. Truly You have provided all this for our good and to showcase Your creativity in nature.

Lord, help me teach my children to appreciate what You've given us. Help me demonstrate good stewardship in our particular town, state, and nation. Give me creative ideas for how to model conserving the gifts of nature You've provided. Please alert me when there's an opportunity to remind my kids that all they see is from Your bountiful hand—and to be thankful.

Truly, Lord, I am grateful.

FATHERING THE FATHERLESS

Father of the fatherless and protector of
widows is God in his holy habitation.
PSALM 68:5-6

A great Christian dad is a treasure to be shared. That is, you can be an influential Christian dad to some of your children's fatherless friends or fatherless children in your church. Become the kind of dad who includes others who may never have an opportunity to go camping or shoot some hoops or learn how to build a bookshelf with a father. Sometimes, someone just being like a dad with them means a lot to a fatherless child.

Lord, I look to You as a paternal role model. You are not only my Father, but a true father to those without earthly dads. Once in a while You bring kids my way who are fatherless for all intents and purposes. Sometimes it's because their own fathers have failed to be there for them. Being a dad to my own children is a high calling, but Lord, when You send others my way who need fatherly affirmation, help me see their need and respond as You respond. Yes, give me a heart for the fatherless. I will help with any small or large effort I can.

Random Acts of Kindness

When you give to the needy, do not let your left hand know what your right hand is doing.
Matthew 6:3

Dads, teach your children the joy of doing good deeds for others anonymously. And on occasion, you can model this behavior by doing a good deed anonymously for them (though the twinkle in your eye is sure to give you away).

Lord, of all the many things I need to teach and model for my kids, surely giving to others anonymously is near the top of the list. Kids, by nature, are mostly takers, not givers. It comes naturally for them to want to receive gifts rather than give them.

Help me show my children that true happiness comes from giving, not getting. Show me opportunities to demonstrate this by helping them perform a random act of kindness without the recipient knowing who the giver is. May my children feel the joy in so doing—and so may I.

Ordinary Dads Can Change the World— One Child at a Time

The LORD will fulfill his purpose for me; your steadfast love, O LORD, endures forever. Do not forsake the work of your hands.
PSALM 138:8

What would our world look like in 20 years if every Christian dad did his part in raising God-loving, praying, mature believers in Christ? It would revolutionize our country and the world. Of course, you can't be a dad to every other child in the nation or world, but you can be that kind of dad to your children. Accept the challenge to be an exceptional Christian dad for your kids.

Father, thank You for the purpose You have for me in being a dad. Thank You for Your steadfast love. Thank You for my children, the work of Your hands. You have fashioned them in the womb and delivered them to me and their mother to parent with a purpose. I pray I will raise them to be adults who matter. Adults who affect their world for good, not for evil.

Lord, rest Your hand on my children today and always. And rest Your hand on me as I bring them up to love You.

A Safe Man

Take no part in the unfruitful works of
darkness, but instead expose them.
EPHESIANS 5:11

We live in dangerous times for children. Some men take advantage of them or other innocents. The reputation of manhood itself suffers with reports of yet another man who has violated a child or a woman. We can help change the reputation of men by vowing in all ways and in all situations to be *safe* men—men and dads who will not only not violate another person, but who will act as defenders of those preyed upon by evil men.

Heavenly Father, give me eyes to see the need to protect and defend innocence. May those who know me consider me to be a man they can count on, a trustworthy man who is a *safe* man. I pray that Your Holy Spirit will empower me to speak up, step up, and man up to stop abuse and violence against women and children. Help me model Christian manhood for my children and their friends. Show me how to enlist other men to be safe men, men who love You and love Your people. Raise up a generation of true men; strong of spirit, soul, and body.